CAMP UNALAYEE

IN CELEBRATION OF 75 YEARS

Place of Friends

Copyright © Priestman Books, 2024
ISBN 978-1-946730-31-2
All stories, poems and artwork are published with the permission of the writers and/or artists.

CONTENTS

Introduction	ix
1. Remembering Unalayee, 1949 *Bob Fuchigami*	1
2. Josephine Duveneck—Camp Unalayee Connections 1949-1950's and Beyond? *Eric Flint*	4
3. The Early Days, 1950's *Corrinne Wolcott Fitch*	7
4. Remote Places, 1960's *Ron Demele*	9
5. Memories of Camp Unalayee, 1961-62 *Russell Van Dyke*	12
6. Unalayee Memories, 1962 *Mary Lux (nee Arnautoff)*	16
7. Vespers, 1964 *Jim Thurber*	18
8. 50 years of Camp U, 1967-2017 *Lynn Meyerson Parker*	19
9. Gifts From The Mountain, 1970 *Bob Strickler*	22
10. Future Boss Man Riding Shotgun, 1970 *Curtis Koppel*	24
11. A Friend Like No Other, Part 1, 1970 & Beyond *Curtis Koppel*	27
12. Friends Like No Others, Part 2, 1970's and Beyond *Curtis Koppel*	30
13. Two Memories, 1970's *Melanie Johnson*	32
14. The First Unalayee Hiking Tribe, 1970 *John Markoff*	34
15. Unalayee's Trucks 1970's-2000's *Tom Bouye*	37
16. The Sweat Lodge, 1970's-2010's *Jessie Camp*	38
17. First Time I Ever, 1972 *Caroline Cooke Carney*	42
18. Spiderman's WFA Reflections, And Other Memories at Camp Unalayee, Place of Friends, 1972-2024 *Tom Halderman, aka Spiderman*	43
19. Hike to Rush Creek Lake, 1973 *Dave McClellen*	46

20. My First Summer at Unalayee, 1974 *Fred Lifton*	47
21. James and the Bear, 1974	49
22. Lantern Man, 1975 *Tom Marquette*	63
23. Rattlesnakes, 1975 *Chris Williams*	66
24. First Summer, 1977 *Walter Chuck*	68
25. I Get By With a Little Help From My Friends, 1977 *Ned Hardwood*	70
26. The Birth Of Gonzo, 1978 *Heather Steele*	72
27. Life as a Central Brat, 1980's-1990's *Becca Fitch Eastman*	76
28. Statue with a Layover, the OG Way, 1980's *Fred Lifton*	78
29. Unalayee Campfires, 1980's-2000's *Jessie Camp*	80
30. Where's Becca? 1980's-90's *Corrine Fitch*	85
31. Choice Hike with Lynn Meyerson Parker and Ed Keifer, 1981 *Donja Blokker*	88
32. The Incomplete History of Camp Unalayee T-shirts, 1981 *Wade Larsen*	91
33. The Cooler, 1981 *Sarah Priestman*	95
34. Vamanos a la playa con Camp Unalayee! 1981 *Eric Gilbert*	98
35. Junk Food Dreams, 1982 *Brian Frank*	100
36. The Hephalump, 1982 *Larry Parker*	102
37. Camp Scott Mountain/Unalayee First Session, 1983 *Walter Chuck*	104
38. CIT Tribe Hike Snow Year, 1983 *Walter Chuck*	106
39. Camp Unalayee and The California Wilderness Act of 1984 *Jay Watson*	108
40. Ode to an Era, 1985 *Heather Scharlack*	110
41. Camp Unalayee, 1987 *Nancy Record (Raven's Mom)*	112
42. Remembering Women's Week, 1980's-90's *Jessie Camp*	114
43. Women's Week Memories, 1990's *Diane Richardson*	118
44. Lightning! 1989 *Ben Salzburg*	121

45. Central Brat Memories, 1990-1996   122
Sarah Camp

46. The Campers From Japan, 1990's-2000's   124
Lowell Fitch

47. Ode to the Sacredness of a Unalayee Childhood, 1992   131
Mneesha Gellman

48. Hiking Tribe Song, 1993   134
Tara Austen Weaver

49. The First and Only Unalayee High Sierra Hiking Tribe, Yet! 1997   136
Tom Bouye

50. The Super Gonzo, 1997   139
Ben Salzburg

51. Unalayee Campfires, 1999   142
Brendan Moroso

52. Beware of Bears Who Love Chocolate Bars, 2000   143
Ismael "Mayo" Cruz

53. Camp Shirts, 2000   145
Nicole LaRiviere

54. One Sweet Memory, 2001 or 2002   148
Martha Stryker

55. CampU Memories, 2002-2003   150
Phil Lee

56. To Mill Creek and Back Again, With a Kayak, 2004   152
Galen Camp

57. Family Week, 2005   155
Nana Connie

58. Gonzo Girl, 2006   158
Becca Fitch Eastman

59. Visit With a Lot Owner, 2012   162
Gail Williams

60. Lowell Day Poem, 2013   163
Submitted by Jessie Camp, who is uncertain of its original author

61. Operation Stealth Cow, 2014   165
Dara Noonan

62. CIT Ditch Day, 2017   167
Amanda Harwood

63. The River Complex   169

64. Flash Of Death, 2021   170
Newt Cohen

65. A Gathering of Friends, 2024   172
Lonna Lewis Blodgett

66. 7000 Ways to Say Friend, Part 1, 2024   174
Curtis Koppel

67. 7001 Ways to Say Friend, Part 2, 2024   177
Curtis Koppel

GONE TOO SOON   181

68. Rudy Breuning   182
1962-2022

69. Josh "Sid the Squid" Bodine　184
1964-2017
70. Little Marshy Lake Lot, 1960's　186
Rita Lompa, Submitted by Kim Garcia
71. Sharing a Love for Life Outside　188
James Camp, 1945-2018
72. A Great Game　193
James Camp
73. James Camp　196
74. Scott Cosgrove　197
1964-2016
75. Carmen Diaz　198
1955-2019
76. Caroline Reeves Johnson　200
1948-2016
77. May Our Stories Continue...　202

Mosquito Basin　203

ARTISTS' BIOS

Front cover art by Elsa Neukom, age 13

When I first began coming to Camp, I had very little experience backpacking. Like everybody, I had a tough first year. As I've gotten older, Camp has only gotten more enjoyable, but equally challenging. Through the years of coming here, Camp Unalayee has been an amazing place to delve deeper into backpacking, nature, and the numerous idyllic lakes of the Trinity Alps. The experiences I've had at Camp have had a huge positive impact on my identity. I am very grateful to be a part of Unalayee.

Gone Too Soon art by Larry Parker

A stranger in a strange land, I worked in the amazing Trinity Alps at Camp U in the summer of '82. My children all spent time there at repeated Family Camp weeks and one as a camper/counselor. Now retired, I spend my time between life on the Skagit Bay in Washington state and Kaua'i in Hawai'i. Camp U and my age put me in mind of this poem by Basho:

Not yet become a Buddha

This ancient pine tree

        Dreaming

Inside back cover art by Rose Lee, age 6

Rose has been a camper in training since 4.5 months. Her favorite thing about camp is EVERYTHING.

Back cover art by Taylor Griffin

I started my journey at Camp Unalayee as an 11-year-old camper in 2000. Over the last 24 years, I've held almost every role imaginable, as a camper, CIT, counselor, CIT counselor, program director, assistant director, and "Camp-Unalayee-enthusiast-who-drove-ten-hours-each-way-to-spend-less-than-a-day-up-in-the-basin-one-weekend-before-he-had-to-be-back-at-work-on-Monday." I am incredibly appreciative of the lifelong family and all the memories made in the Trinity Alps, across the country, and around the world. I'm now teaching high school English in Seattle, Washington, which frees up my summers to continue spending time up at the most wonderful place on earth, Camp Unalayee

Dear Friends,

When I learned of the 75th reunion, I knew I wanted to contribute something we could all share to celebrate our anniversary. This anthology is what I came up with. Everybody has a Unalayee story, and now we've got a range of them gathered in one place.

I joined the staff as a last-minute hire in '79. Camp needed to replace Gina Thompson in the food shack (which was impossible), so hired me, an unknown with high-energy restaurant experience and zero miles on the trail. I rode up RT 5 in the green truck with Chris Williams and Lynn Parker, detouring to Sacramento, where we stacked boxes of government cheese onto the flatbed. As we traveled north and I listened to their stories, I fell in love with the community.

We'd arrived to join the opening work-crew. I was industrious, and would do anything, so Chris assigned me to Tom Bouye, which meant we traced the waterlines through the basin, crouching down to secure clamps around the endless spurting leaks, or we jammed cardboard into the "burn barrel," which was how we managed waste back then, or we looped rusted rings around metal biffy frames to hang canvas privacy drapes. Those things were heavy!

And, I worked with Lynn Parker in the old, lantern-lit food shack. We'd unload the truck when it returned from a run to Farrington's, rip open boxes, and pour raisins or rice or macaroni into the white bins that had survived the winter chippies. And with Chris, who leafed through Gina's food shack binder, explaining the day-by-day routine of the job, which was then held by one person, who also went out on the trail. And Carmen, who talked about the kids we'd meet. And James, who, on the staff hike, introduced me to battling manzanita while traversing cross-country.

Every set of instructions I received was really a glorified story. This is how I do it, this is how so-and-so did it wrong, this is the funny thing that someone else once did, this is what we remember. Camp operates, in part, through stories.

Camp has changed since I started. The food shack has lights. The Trinities have the PCT. We no longer set the trash on fire. And, much is also the same: our founding commitment to equity, our reverence for wilderness, our belief in sowing seeds of peace through living in community. Also the same: our love of stories.

This anthology is a celebration of Camp through those stories. The recollections, yes, but also the intermingling of different voices, memories, views. It has been a joy to read each submission and connect with writers and artists as the book took shape. I hope you all enjoy the collection.

Thanks to Mariah and Martha for communications support, and to Curtis,

Jessie, Tom, and Lynn for always being available when I needed fact-checking or cheerleading. We are truly a Place of Friends.

Here's to making more stories in the future!

Sarah Priestman

Food shack, counselor, truck driver, director, Family Camper, volunteer, anthology curator

1

REMEMBERING UNALAYEE, 1949

BOB FUCHIGAMI

Many of you know that Camp Unalayee was conceived and started in 1949 as an experimental interracial Camp for young boys under the guidance of the legendary Josephine Duveneck. The director of Camp Unalayee for the first twelve years was Bruce McNeil, an elementary school teacher in Palo Alto. The Camp was located in the redwoods of the Santa Cruz mountains near Ben Lomond until 1959, when it was moved to its present spot in the Trinities. For those of you who have forgotten the move to the Trinities, I'd like to refresh some memories.

The summer of 1959 was a challenge to say the least. The plan was to have Melvin Stroud, Bob Fuchigami, and "Uncle Ray" Wilson direct the first two sessions of Camp on the Ben Lomond site, and have the third session in the new Camp location in the Trinities.

A contingency plan was to hold the third session in the Sierras if the Trinity site was not ready for campers. To further complicate matters. Bruce was scheduled to be away the first eight weeks of the summer to pursue a masters' degree at Stanford. Fortunately, the first two sessions of Camp in Ben Lomond went rather smoothly.

Meanwhile, things were getting rather hectic for the move to the Trinities for the third session. Bruce had completed his Stanford studies and was working mightily with a small work crew to open a rough road up Tangle Blue creek to the new Camp site on Mosquito Lake. Each day the bulldozer would work its way a little further up the road. One day the dozer lost its front big blade trying to move some huge rocks around to ford the rocks out of Big Marshy Lake. (Incidentally, the blade is still visible in the crack wedged among the rocks. Look for it the next time you are hiking on the road toward Tangle Blue Lake).

A final decision had to be made: Trinities or the Sierras?

The Trinities site was not quite ready. Holes for biffies were still in the process of being dynamited. The bulldozer was still a few miles away from the campsite. The bus company was getting anxious. Parents of the campers were making inquiries about where their children would be going. A decision was made: the Trinities, ready or not.

An agreement was reached with school officials at Trinity Center to allow a group of campers to sleep overnight on their school grounds. The bus went as far as Trinity Center and dropped off the campers and counselors at the school site. As the bulldozer pushed toward Camp, the campers followed with full packs.

In essence, the first five days of the third session were spent getting to the Camp site on Mosquito Lake. The campers literally followed the bulldozer into Camp. Third session of Camp Unalayee was a lesson in survival. Campers had to make their own sleeping quarters under the stars. Water was taken from the stream flowing out of the lake. There was no food shack or nurses' tent or platform for the office. There was only one road in or out and that was so rough that only four wheeled vehicles could make it through. Provisions were trucked in via Trinity Center- not Callahan or Etna because the present road from the summit was non-existent. There was little programming that session except orientation hikes to become familiar with the new environment. One structure was built that summer- a small A frame tool shed. Work was started on several tent platforms and a search was made for a spring that could be developed for a source of water.

Needless to say, the first session of Camp Unalayee on Mosquito Lake was a memorable experience. For all of us who "survived" that summer, it was an exciting time. I remember the day the bulldozer made it into Camp and the first vehicle that followed it. It was a four-wheel drive International panel truck. The truck had been pulling a trailer behind it with a load of camping gear, including some packs and sleeping bags. During the last leg up the road, which traversed the rockpile on the ridge between Shasta point and Tangle Blue, the hitch on the trailer came loose and the trailer with all its contents went crashing over the ridge! At that moment it was apparent to all of us that camping in the Trinities was going to be a once in a lifetime adventure-and it was!

BOB FUCHIGAMI, *Ed.D., was one of Camp Unalayee's original founders. His family was interned at Colorado's Merced Assembly Center, California and Granada (Amache) concentration camp after the bombing of Pearl Harbor. He has been a professor in special education at the Universities of Hawaii and Oregon, and was the Chairman of the Education Department and Dean of Graduate Studies at Sonoma State College.*

Bob is the author of "Amache Remembered." He advocated for the designation of Amache as a National Historic Site, a battle which was won in 2022. He has dedicated his life to working in the areas of peace and social justice, dedicated to keeping the history of Japanese internment camps alive.

2

JOSEPHINE DUVENECK—CAMP UNALAYEE CONNECTIONS 1949-1950'S AND BEYOND?

ERIC FLINT

I am the lead history volunteer at Hidden Villa, "just" down the hill from the Ben Lomond Center on the way towards Los Altos via Skyline, Page Mill and then Moody Road. Our interest in Camp Unalayee was sparked when we recently received two treasured song books used at Josephine Duveneck's Hidden Villa Camp in the 1970's and 1990's. Both credited a Camp Unalayee Songbook. In fact, the 1970 one was "just" the Camp Unalayee songbook (see next page).

Curious, I reached out to your archivists, and I was excited to learn that you are celebrating your 75th anniversary as a camp, much as we at Hidden Villa are celebrating our Centennial of when the Duvenecks first purchased the land in 1924.

Josephine was deeply connected with the Bay Area Quaker community and was an active member of the local American Friends Service Committee (AFSC). Having deep knowledge of children via her decades of experience at the Peninsula School that she helped found in 1925 and having founded her own multi-racial summer camp in 1945 at Hidden Villa (both, much like Camp Unalayee, still running today), she was instrumental in setting up the Camp Unalayee at Ben Lomond in 1949.

Per Dianne Pitman, in John deValcourt's Short History (of the Ben Lomond Center) there is a reference to a June 1949 *"agreement between Lucille Manley and Josephine Duveneck that the latter will operate, through the AFSC, an inter-racial boys camp"*

Josephine was also a regular Christmas letter writer. While we unfortunately don't have a letter from the seminal 1949, in her 1950 Christmas Chronicle she writes:

> "As usual we operated our Summer Camp [ed: i.e. the Hidden Villa] this year - We had 115 children in the course of the 7 weeks. Pretty good lot of kids and counselors. When they get too old to come to Camp [ed. back then by age 12 or 13) they start writing to apply for the job of dishwasher and handyman. You'd be surprised at the competition for this menial position.
>
> Some of the boys went on to the Friend's Camp at Ben Lomond in Santa Cruz Mts., which is for teen-age boys. The place is still relatively underdeveloped, but some good things happened to the 18-20 boys who participated last year. [ed i.e. 1949]"

We have also learned that at least some early Camp Unalayee board meetings and fundraising events were held at Hidden Villa's Main House in the 50's. I was also recently participating in an oral history of a Hidden Villa Camper/Councilor (Tom Lederer) and was surprised to hear that after he "aged out" of Hidden Villa camp, he (and his brother) went onto be a Counselor In Training (CIT) at Camp Unalayee for 5 years sometime in the 60's, helping to build out the early Mosquito Lake area, prior to returning to be a Counselor at Hidden Villa when he was in college.

Also according to Tom Buoye, "Many of HV and Josephine's ideas about summer camps as described in her autobiography, 'Life on Two Levels', for example unstructured time, are still a part of Unalayee's program"

The early (and ongoing) links between Camp Unalayee and Hidden Villa are clearly deep and strong, and we are looking forward to working with all of you to add more to the joint history of both camps.

ERIC FLINT, *Lead History @ Hidden Villa Volunteer. When not haunting archives, Eric likes to read science fiction, walk the dog and go to Farmers Markets. If anybody has memories of connections between HV and Camp Unalayee, we'd love to hear about them! You can reach me at History@hiddenvilla.org*

Special thanks to Carolyn Chan, HV Camp Counselor (1976-1979) for loaning us her copy of the 1970's "Hidden Villa" song book that started all this.

3

THE EARLY DAYS, 1950'S
CORRINNE WOLCOTT FITCH

My parents were both really active in the beginning. One of the documents that Curtis has found has a list of the committees for the formation of Camp, and that has my mother's name on it. My dad was very active in helping to build the buildings up at Camp, and then he and a bunch of other guys put in the water line. They were there at the very beginning.

They were part of the Quaker Meeting community that started the original program in Ben Lomond. Through the Quakers, they were very good friends with Josephine and Frank Duveneck. Actually, the Duvenecks lived right over the hill from us in Los Altos Hills.

When I was growing up, my family was caretaking a massive piece of property for a woman who was a countess. This was our landlady. My mom had put an ad in the paper offering to be a caretaker. The ad said she was living with four kids in a 900 square foot house in Palo Alto and she needed more space, so was there anyone out there that lived in the hills and wanted to have a caretaker for their land or for their house?

So, this woman, this countess, answered that ad. My mom packed up all the kids and we all went out to see the place and the countess fell in love with my mom and said, "Ok, it's yours."

So now this house was ours to caretake for as long as we'd like.

I was four when we moved up there, so that would have been about 1953. They would have started the Camp in Ben Lomond by then. We left when I was 16. We lived there for 12 years. My entire childhood. We were on 250 acres, and it was still undeveloped in the 1950s. I could ride my horse over to Hidden Villa. I worked as a housekeeper at Hidden Villa at one point, too.

This woman, this countess, had land all over the United States and in Europe, but at some point, we had to move away – something about the taxes. This house was an old stagecoach stop with 17 rooms. People tried to save it once all the development started in Los Altos Hills, but that didn't work. The land is still beautiful, though, if you don't know what used to be there.

CORINNE WAS a Unalayee camper since the 1960s, and joined the staff in 1970, the same summer she met Lowell. They later married and raised their daughters, Beth and Becca, at Camp. Corinne started the Women's Hike, played guitar and led songs around the campfire for generations of campers, and has been a much-loved member and leader of the Unalayee community through the decades.

4

REMOTE PLACES, 1960'S
RON DEMELE

As we crossed the ridge and headed north past eagle peak, then off trail into the manzanita, headed for lonely west boulder lake. at first sight of the lake, the basin felt a little eerie to us. we stumbled over to the rocky shore. I dropped my pack and headed for some shade away from the lake.

we had planned to swim and fish, but for unknown reasons we felt strange approaching the water. along the shoreline an old campfire ring was spotted. it was old style...very large were the rocks, and large was the circle. inside that circle contained a big rock covering a mound of ancient garbage. pealing back the treasure, I found an old, rusted tobacco tin from the 1950s. a red, king albert tin with his picture on it also in the pile were plenty of fish hooks...now rusted and unusable. I lifted the can and noticed an ancient Burgermeister" beer can!

we made Camp in a flat spot not too far from the lake. we all rounded up some dry manzanita wood to burn for the evening blaze. we set up our Camp nearby and set out our sleeping bags, cooked up some easy mac and cheese, and stoked the fire as evening set in.

so here is what I remember about the evening. as it grew increasingly dark, we hooped and hollered enjoying the echo that was made off the granite rocks on the other side of the lake. hlllllllow. heyyyy yoooouuuu. one- part and two-part echo harmonies kept us entertained as it grew late. what fun to shout at the mountains, sitting around the fire as night engulfed our Campsite in the mild summer evening. full lung bellows soon followed and were content at finding true wilderness with no one to bother. one by one we got tired of this activity and retreated to our cozy sleeping bags. the moon was up, and nearly full.

then, suddenly, it began across the lake high up into the rock cliffs.

up on the rocky peak we could hear rocks sliding down into other rocks. our ears were fully open now. occasionally deer, bear or humans can cause rocks to slide and be audible that far away. this sound was big. It was like a large rockslide set off by something. this sounded like someone or something very large walking across very loose rock causing rolling rocks to tumble down the steep rockslide scree below the peak. soon we all tuned into this event still convinced it was a natural occurrence caused by the forces around us. rocks do slide. animals move around at night. maybe it was the echo effect.

now, screams came from across the lake and bounced back into our Camp. just below the peak came the sound of a scream so scary we all froze. it was the sound of a murder just on the other side of the lake.

oh my god...there it is again we murmured, almost too frightened to speak loudly. a mountain lion? it came from up in the rocks and repeated again. it was horrible. it was a sound that ripped right through me. we all grabbed our sleeping bags and moved up to the Camp fire.

"what the hell was that?

another large branch was put on the fire, causing it to bring back a bright high flame, snapping and roaring back from the glow. but it was not over. more screams clear and loud tore into the night air. loud high pitched and deathly... we all thought; mountain lion.

too many rocks sliding... that was something bigger and heavier. now there was something new. the sound of very large rocks were beginning to roll down the rock slide across the lake. giant boulders bounced down the peak side scree... boom booom booom.

someone or something was throwing the large boulders every few minutes down the slope. a few more murderous screams, then silence. then the rocks crashed and rolled their way down the dark slope toward the lake, this time, one at a time. Sasquatch?

we were all experienced hikers and backpackers. we knew the alps, but now had no idea what this terrifying event was all about. no other humans were anywhere near this lake basin. mountain lions would not do this...

they are too shy and afraid of humans, just like bears in this area. bears in this country look like big dogs and are not a problem for humans. deer are too frail for anything like this behavior. natural earth slides do not continuously keep up this activity for hours.

sasquatch?

this series of terror carried on for hours. near morning, after staying up almost all night feeding the fire, we feel asleep. I dreamt that a big lion had come into Camp and circled our Camp.

in the morning light I looked for footprints, but nothing remained, only memories of screams and rocks rolling.

we cleaned up Camp at first light, and put out the fire.

we packed up all our gear and our sleeping bags.

as we looked back at the lake before launching again into the manzanita-strangled ridge, we loaded in the artifacts from the fire ring trash, and wondered had they too left in a hurry many years ago?

RON DEMELE IS a retired media teacher at College of the Siskiyous, book author (pacific crest trail...mountain encounters of a wilderness ranger), 3 years Camp Counselor, 2 years Board of Directors in late 60s early 70s.

5

MEMORIES OF CAMP UNALAYEE, 1961-62
RUSSELL VAN DYKE

I attended Camp twice, probably in 1961 and 1962, when I was 11 and 12 years old. This was only a couple of years after the Camp had been run by the Friends, and many of the Camp traditions reflected this.

The trip up to Camp was an all day bus trip. We met in Palo Alto and drove up old highway 99 to Redding. It was always a very long and hot trip. We always stopped in Willits at the A & W Root Beer stand for lunch, a treat that we looked forward to.

Once we got near Camp, the bus would stop at the start of the dirt road that led up to Camp. We threw all of our gear into the back of two flat-bed trucks and then all piled in on top for the bumpy ride into Camp. The trucks were old and rickety. One was named the "Gray Ghost"; I don't remember the name of the second one.

Once in Camp, we found our tribes and set up Camp. At that time, the sexes were segregated: the boys were on the left side of the road (facing up the valley towards the lake) and the girls were on the right, near Mosquito Lake. We all camped out under the stars and food was cooked over wood fires - I understand that this hasn't changed. Water was distributed by a series of black hoses which ran all over the ground. Each tribe chose a name. The name of my tribe one year was "The Minihoonies," which refers to the Hawaiian equivalent of a Leprechaun.

Much of the food we ate was dehydrated; a brand called "Dry Lite" stands out. It wasn't well liked and there was a Camp song about it, to the tune of "Oleanna":

If you want to have some fun, to Unalayee you must go,
   have a plate of Dry Lite, kill you in a week or so,
U-na U-na layee, U-na U-na lay-ee-ee
U-na U-na, U-na U-na, U-na U-na lay-ee-ee

There was also plenty of fruit punch that we made in large metal buckets known as "bug juice," which was sweet and well loved. It lived up to its name by attracting all sorts of flying insects.

Camp routine started early in the morning with our counselors somehow getting us out of

bed. Before breakfast, we had "Morning Thoughts" at the campfire circle. At this brief meeting, there were several short readings. We also sang songs, such as "No Man is an Island":

No man is an island,
   No man stands alone.
   Each man's joys are joys for me,
   Each man's tears are my own.

After breakfast and Camp clean-up, we had morning activities. A popular one was the crafts shack, which was down by the dirt road leading out of Camp. My favorite activity was to collect pieces of manzanita root, which could be sanded to a smooth surface and then waxed. This brings out the beautiful grain pattern of the wood and results in a very pretty piece. I still have one around somewhere. We also made belts and other things out of leather.

Lunch usually consisted of rye crisp with peanut butter and jam - and of course bug juice. After lunch we often went swimming in Mosquito Lake. I recall mud and grass and good times but fortunately no mosquitoes. This may be a selective loss of memory as a result of the passage of time.

Other afternoons, we explored the basin in which the Camp was located. I remember a day hike up a very steep talus slope over the ridge on the right side of the valley, above the girls Camp and the lake. I believe that there was a lake just over the other side of the ridge.

One of the counselors developed "water on the knee" on the hike, and had difficulty getting down the steep slope. I recall collecting pennyroyal, which we used to make a fine mint tea. I was also very impressed with the pitcher plants we found growing in the wet stream beds in the meadows. We were impressed with the bugs being digested by the plant. We were taught a little rock climbing by one of the counselors by the name of Sharsmith (son of Carl Sharsmith, Yosemite ranger and professor at San Jose State). He kept his climbing gear in a cave on the ridge above the boys Camp, which was known as Sharsmith's Cave. It was apparently very difficult to get up into the cave, so the campers couldn't get into the climbing gear. I have asked my son Daryl about Sharsmith's Cave, but apparently it is no longer a recognized landmark.

In the evening before dinner (as I recall, about 6 PM), we had Vespers on the ridge to the left of Camp, above the boys Camp. We would sit on the rocks in the quiet and watch the colors from the setting sun on Mount Shasta. It was always very peaceful and beautiful - one of the special things about Camp. At least, it was usually quiet and peaceful; I remember once that we got a stern lecture about "passing gas at vespers."

After dinner, there was a campfire. I remember vaguely that there were skits and songs - probably lots of silliness. Among the songs that I first learned there, the one that stands out is the "Ballad of Springhill" by Ian McCall, which is about a mining disaster in Nova Scotia. It made a lasting impression on me. We also sent inexperienced campers on the usual search for a left-handed monkey wrench or a pair of snipes. These were always great fun for everyone except the poor campers doing the searching. I vaguely recall some midnight raids on the girl's Camp, but the details are fortunately lost in time.

A highlight of the camp was an overnight hike. As I recall, we took one three-day hike. This was well before the days of fancy camping gear; many campers made their backpack out of a pair of jeans! The gear was stuffed in, the waist opening closed off with string, and the legs wrapped around the shoulders to serve as the straps. I assume that the cuffs were pinned to the seat. This was obviously an uncomfortable way to carry gear, but it was all that most of us had. Only the counselors had real backpacks. As a result of this and other limitations, our trips were much less ambitious than those of today. No "Gonzos" for us. I believe that my first overnight was to Tango Blue Lake.

My most memorable trip was one in which we climbed Eagle Peak the first day, and explored an old gold mine on the second, while hiking down into Callahan. I found a carbide miners head lamp in the mine, which I took home and was able to make work, using calcium carbide. We also caught and killed a rattlesnake, which was cooked in oil and we all had a bite. Tasted like chicken, I suppose. In retrospect, we probably should not have either explored the mine, nor killed the snake. We camped near town and then hiked back up to Camp on the third day. We were very proud of ourselves for hiking so far, without a layover day. I remember that the counselors gave me an old metal (a marksman metal as I recall) as an award for making that hike. Apparently I was having some trouble on the hike, and the blue jeans pack didn't help. I really appreciated the metal, and kept it for many years.

Of course, a great day was when care packages arrived from home: cookies and candy and such. I like to think that we all shared what we got with each other.

I have a few other isolated memories. I remember the tent which sold supplies and sweat shirts - I very badly wanted a Camp sweatshirt with a hood and a pocket in front for your hands. I think that I finally did get one. I still have a green Unalayee patch, with the 5 squares on it. I also recall that the camp had a shortwave radio in a small silver trailer, which it used to communicate with Palo Alto.

Leaving Camp was the reverse of coming in: early in the morning, we tossed our gear into the back of the trucks, in we climbed, and off we went down the dirt road to the busses. It was a long hot drive back to Palo Alto. One year, one of the trucks was broken, so half of the campers, including myself, were driven down to the buses the evening before, where we camped. I remember it as quite an adventure. Since it was much lower than Camp, we were worried about rattlesnakes. I suppose Camp was too high for rattlesnakes; I don't recall seeing any.

Several months into the school year, there was a reunion for the campers in the Palo Alto area. I remember getting together in a multi-purpose room somewhere and reliving our Camp adventures. I am sure that there were songs and stories; there may have been phots and slides; I don't recall the details.

My two years at Camp were an important part of my growing up, which I still remember fondly. It was there that my lifelong interest in camping, hiking, and the outdoors became firmly established. The caring humanist philosophy of the camp also came through and I am grateful for this as well.

I ATTENDED CAMP TWICE, probably in 1961 and 1962, when I was 11 and 12 years old. I am partially retired, living in Washington State after having taught and done research at the Tulane School of Medicine in New Orleans for 38 years. I am still involved in a long-term study of children living with HIV and those exposed at birth to HIV who were not infected. I am happy to be back on the West Coast.

6

UNALAYEE MEMORIES, 1962
MARY LUX (NEE ARNAUTOFF)

Unalayee was the first and only summer camp I attended, and I still have wonderful memories.

I remember Vespers, sitting over the lake and hearing John Dunne's "No Man is an Island" poem, for the first time, which as you see left a lasting impression. We also learned the song *Dona, Dona, Dona*, which I recently taught to a group of friends who only knew the Hebrew translation.

I remember making a "backpack" from a pair of jeans.

Writing home to my Mom that I'd made a new friend, and her reply that I had been friends with her when we were only 2 years old in the student housing at UC Berkeley.

The "tent" we had to hastily put up with a rope between 2 trees and a tarp thrown over it, when it started raining one night.

But, the most traumatic memory was the ride down the mountain on the last day in a cattle truck with a tarp thrown over the top against the rain. The tarp would sag from the rain and we would stand up to push the water over the sides. At some point the truck skidded in the mud and it was decided that we had to walk the rest of the way down. It was muddy and wet, I remember my shoe getting stuck in the mud.

When we got down and back to "civilization" the first news we heard was that Marilyn Manroe had died.

Until this day, my favorite times are the hikes in mountains like the Trinity Alps. My husband and I are avid hikers and have hiked all over the world. I credit the seeds of this love in the incredible two weeks at Unalayee so long ago!

· · ·

I ATTENDED Camp in August 1962. I am retired, but still working part time as a registered nurse in my kibbutz clinic. I have lived in Israel since 1968.

7

VESPERS, 1964

JIM THURBER

My second year at Camp Unalayee, 1964, we were sitting at Vespers point. Silently we waited for our Camp Director, Andy Anderson, while watching Mount Shasta turning a brilliant pink in the setting sun.

Suddenly the silence was broken by a tremendous, truly magnificent breaking of wind. The perpetrator . . . unknown. The barking sounds which sounded very much like bubble wrap hitting a running jet engine, seemed to be gathering strength whilst echoing off the rocks and trees.

Nobody moved. Nobody said a sound. We saw Andy coming up the trail. Did he hear it? What would he say? Nobody had a clue. I suspect we were all terrified.

Andy stepped forward, paused and began the Vespers. He said, *"This reminds me. Many years ago, a wise man said, 'If you're going to do anything, do it really well."*

The entire Camp dissolved in uproariously laughter as Andy continued. *"Time for Campfire. Let's go."*

And we did.

I was a camper from 1963 thru 1967. Andy Anderson and Warren Hayward were my Camp Directors. Paul and Mary Beard were most influential.

8

50 YEARS OF CAMP U, 1967-2017

LYNN MEYERSON PARKER

1967: I spent most of my time in the nurses' shack, homesick beyond belief. Major jake. Took my two hikes to the Tea Cups and Big Marshy. Went snipe hunting and held the end of the wash table for rinsing. Yet cried when it was time to go home?!?

1968: Got ambitious and went to Tangle Blue and Big Marshy. Still a jake. Premiered the *Crisco: But It's Shortening!* skit.

1969: Made lifelong friends. Got a glimpse into what a creative life, well lived, might look like by observing hippie counselors in their natural environment. Log Lake and Doe Lake were my stretch goals. Made it! Missed the moon landing, oh well.

1970: Hung out with the work crew while they dug biffies. Tried the craft shack (not much of a visual artist) and decided my best and highest activity was hanging out at the waterfront. Grizzly Lake and Middle Boulder hikes.

1971: Saved-up babysitting money to be able to go to two sessions. Went to Bear and Little Bear, down bushwhacking and up the chute. Lived to tell the tale (barely).

1972: Tried making Swiss Hiker's Cereal and eating it at home. Apparently, it requires many hours on the trail to actually be edible.

1973: Cried when singing *Give me a Rose in the Wintertime*. Hiked down the road to the Y to get drunk for my first time with a work crew buddy. It wasn't on Camp property, so it was ok, right? Lost my favorite galvanized metal hiking spoon.

1974: Did the famous hike to Kangaroo Lake! And the infamous fu@#ing on the lake flower identification hike. Left from Camp to walk the not-yet-created Pacific Crest Trail with my friend Martha down to Lassen. (Yes, we got lost.)

1975: Wanted to be a counselor. Didn't make it. Major angst and disappointment.

1976: Didn't go to Camp again. Sulky baby.

1977: Got my Water Safety Instructor certification so they would have to take me. It worked! My spoon was returned to me, after going around the world with Ed!

1979: Rode up to Camp with the amazing Sarah Priestman. Lifetime besties, commence!

1980: Many nights packing food in the food shack while discussing life philosophy. Skinniest I ever was! Somewhere in here was the heroic cooler build; a nighttime extravaganza of concrete and men working by lamplight.

1981: Sent my soon-to-be husband up to experience Camp as the nurse, after giving him a haircut (how hard can it be?). Donja said: "either that's a political statement, or the worst haircut I've ever seen." He liked Camp, but thought the culture weird.

1982-1985: Attended women's week, several times, I think. Lots of time hanging, reading, enjoying the lack of patriarchy. What would men's week look like? I envision lots of spitting and chainsaws, but that's hardly fair.

1985-1990: Busy parenting twins. No memories of this time. I think I didn't sleep much...

1990-1997: Family Camp adventures with twins, husband, lots of making weird stuff in the craft shack (Lanyards, anyone? Flower blueprints? Sad carved spoons?)

1998: Brought my five-month old baby Calvin up to Camp, nursing him on a tent platform deck while fearfully listening to bears marauding through Central.

2000: Sent my teen-age twins up to Camp. It didn't work its magic; we're all different, I guess.

2008: Sent late-in-life baby Calvin to Camp: It took!

2009-2014: Drove down through Oregon and Washington to Camp to drop Calvin off at Camp. Went back two weeks later to pick him up. Good thing I enjoy road trips!

2015: Met a woman at a beach on the Big Island who asked me to watch her stuff while she snorkeled. She was from Ashland, and her son went to Camp Unalayee! We arranged to fly Calvin down and have her drive the last two hours to Camp. Serendipity!

2016-2017: Calvin became a counselor, got a tattoo of a Pika on his arm in the craft shack (to his mother's horror), and I patted myself on the back having successfully passed down the love of Camp gene!

That's 50 years, and I'm still involved and in love with the power and the magic of Camp U. Long may it give kids a foundation of confidence, connection and community.

LYNN PARKER'S 50 years at Camp include being a camper, women's week attendee, Family Camp attendee, counselor, and volunteer. She is retired, and splitting her time between Kauai and La Conner Washington, playing pickleball, reading, walking, birding, whale watching, turtle protecting, cooking.

9

GIFTS FROM THE MOUNTAIN, 1970
BOB STRICKLER

It was 1970. I had a BA in psychology, recreation therapy and child development and had worked at a psychiatric hospital - mostly with adolescents. I was volunteering for room and board at Walden House, a residential treatment place for recovering heroin addicts in a glorious but very faded old Victorian just off of the Haight in San Francisco. I also had a job at one of those tacky employment agencies - really no money. My girlfriend had just informed me that I was not the right guy. Somehow, I had contracted arsenic poisoning and wound up with a miserable neuropathy. It was really time for a serious change.

At the agency I found an ad for a Camp director. I had worked seasonally at summer Camps and had been a senior counselor. I called, they interviewed me (a full board - kind of intimidating), they called and hired me. I accepted. Ok - that's a change.

Curtis was there, and I said that I would need some help and he stepped up. He was ready for a change too. OK- that's good.

The Board was quite clear that I was not to hire ANY former staff. Something had come down the previous season. They were deliberately very vague, but one can imagine.

OK so now I will be flying blind in the wilderness with some 100 campers and 30 odd staff. Ok - that's a challenge.

So I went about hiring staff, I was lucky. They turned out to be a wonderful mix of new people, some were ex-campers, some had prior experience in other camps, some had none, some were incredible volunteers who dug biffies and magically tended to decaying structures out of thin air as there was no money, and I hired some friends who I knew I could count on. And some could make music! So now we could sing around campfires. OK - that's wonderful.

Now the real issue was - how do you run a wilderness Camp if you don't know the traditions, songs, skits, culture - or even where the trails and lakes are? Ok - that's a challenge.

Fortunately there were some counselors who had been campers, Board members who visited - (watching us closely) - and some who had been there for years like Mary Beard who ran the food shack all summer and Margo Edwards, and Candy Steel who were camp nurses. They all shared and helped me and our completely naive staff pull it together. But most of all it was the campers themselves who taught us how to have a real Unalayee Camp program. An absolutely marvelous mix that came together to again prove that this was indeed a Place of Friends.

After a couple of seasons it became apparent to me that Unalayee was again ripe for change and that I should not be part of it. I resigned and Unalayee went on again in its own transitional way. It has done this many times over the years. I think that Unalayee is much like a living being, It grows, learns, and changes. And it is always guided as "A Place Of Friends" that has the power to challenge and change the lives of campers and staff. Those who are entrusted now and in the future carry with them the responsibility to see that it is always that way.

I learned a lot about people, organizations, and mostly myself. It transformed me.

Unalayee, I thank you.

My experience at Unalayee gave me the courage to take risks and live some of my dreams. I built a geodesic dome off the grid in a remote valley outside of Weaverville. Eventually married and raised a boy and a girl. Wood heat, gravity fed spring water, a garden, the whole nine yards. I earned a master's degree, got an LCSW and worked for community mental health and then retired.

I now live in Tucson. I was widowed a few years ago. I have a lady friend who lives down the street. We like to find live music and dance, we travel and Camp as much as we are able. I visit old friends - some of them from Camp and some that go back 60 years. I am very thankful.

10

FUTURE BOSS MAN RIDING SHOTGUN, 1970

CURTIS KOPPEL

We started what would become a long journey from the day we met. We were just 15 in 1962. Lowell and I would share countless adventures in the years to come. We journeyed without benefit of a guide or preparation. We would hitchhike 500 miles on a dime. We visited Haight-Ashbury in search of a simpler life. The summer of love remains an iconic moment in our past. Our preferred destination, however, was south, seeking tropical surf in Mexico for months at a time.

In 1969 we set out on an adventure living in my $100 36 hp 1957 VW bus. This journey would take us from Mexico to Vancouver Island along the coast. We were frugal to a fault and carefree with our time. Friends had welcomed us to stay at their place on the Russian River. We had met surfing in San Blas the previous year. If you could call it a conflict, we did have a problem. Money was short. Our box of Roman Meal and bread took priority over buying a dollar of gas.

We were flexible so I would seek work solo. I would take the van back to the city while Lowell was working as a shepherd. In the right place at the right time, I found work the first day. A warehouse supplied small family delis all over SF and I had just the van to deliver. I was exploring how to drive and park like a local while eating good and meeting great people.

I met John, a founding director at the Haight Ashbury Free Clinic. It was the first of its kind in the Nation. I would volunteer evening hours observing John's methods for solution focused brief therapy. Years later after graduating from

Berkeley and returning from Sweden, I would train with John at his Cypress Institute as a LMFT intern in psychotherapy. *(Another story)*

At that same time in 1969 the Alcatraz protest was heating up with Native Americans of All Tribes (IAT) and their supporters occupying Alcatraz Island. The Occupation of Alcatraz and the Free Clinic were both supported by donations and volunteers. I supported the movement and actively advocated for change.

The organizations supporting the Alcatraz occupation required hundreds of free hands. My van could deliver supplies to the dock, and I was familiar with double parking anywhere in SF. That was also a time when a VW Bus always stopped for hitchhikers and riders would often help me load supplies. You would see that 57 VW bus everywhere. It was always on the move. My favorite back bumper sticker proudly read: "**I might be slow, but I'm in front of you.**"

When I first met Wilma, we were working shoulder to shoulder. She possessed a remarkable ability to motivate all of us while confidently ensuring every necessary supply reached the island. Wilma would anchor me with increased enthusiasm for change. I recognized that my personal financial conflicts were unmistakably out of touch. Fortunately, operating at a loss was not new to me. I was clearly profiting from new counsel. With certainty my experiences with Wilma Mankiller and John Frykman had moved me to new chapters in my book titled: *Operating at a Loss for Fun and Profit.*

Those associations helped provide a foundational backdrop for what was about to change my life forever. I had wanted to visit a friend I had known from San Diego State. Bob was working and living at Walden House just off Haight Street near the Clinic. We had stories to share but neither of us imagined how dramatically our lives were about to change after that evening.

Bob described the events consuming his time. Walden House treated heroin addiction and was not an easy place to work or live. As much as I was learning on the streets of SF, I was far happier surfing with Lowell. We were all searching for future horizons.

Bob had interviewed for a new job. Something about Outdoor Education with a nonprofit. He said it was a long shot but just then a coworker interrupted him with a call on the office phone. He returned with a changed expression to say it was a board member offering him the position and he accepted. Bob said he would need assistance and soon.

Lowell and I were unquestionably back on the road again, but our journey was taking a big turn. With Lowell riding shotgun, we would make our way to Tofino BC and back in record time before starting to work. Bob Strickler would be the new Camp Unalayee director. I would be assistant Navi-Guesser. *That's a person who guesses; especially someone who can make a reasonable prediction extrapolating from limited information.*

It would be no small task finding staff and preparing for Camp, so Bob and I had our work cut out. Having gathered an entirely fresh staff for the summer of 1970, I would be in the right place again at the right time. A 'Place of Friends' at Camp Unalayee in the Trinity Alps with Lowell. I would be going home to a place I had never been.

I would forever return to Camp. Lowell would forever stay. He would weave his magic at Camp Unalayee. The Boss Man riding shotgun storied a lifetime of treasures on our journey. Only Boss Man can best tell those tales in his profoundly exceptional way.

Curtis Koppel is still *in the lineup. You can find him at findingcurtis@gmail.com*

Involvement as Camp staff in 1970 left a lasting impact on my life. Generations of families return, creating a tight-knit community. The commitment of friends and supporters ensures that Unalayee provides a unique experience for youth, fostering growth and lasting memories.It is a joy to be a part of the enduring legacy of Camp Unalayee!

11

A FRIEND LIKE NO OTHER, PART 1, 1970 & BEYOND

CURTIS KOPPEL

James Camp was a beloved and loving friend. James knew something special about the simple truth. He showed us what caring is about. He was a self-taught naturalist with a unique and unparalleled philosophy of life. James would be a friend like no other.

I had only been at Camp long enough that first summer to recognize how much there was to do. When we arrived that summer of 1970, there was not an empty biffy in Camp. There were more resources tied up in hose clamps than hose. Tent platforms had been twisted like pretzels and the old food shack structure was listing.

I was checking the status of new biffies. Allan and Alf were digging one while John and Gary were digging another. It was early in a race, and they were hard at it. Their teams were competing to see who could dig the deepest biffy and how fast they could dig them before moving on to the next two.

It was a perfect beginning when making a new friend at a 'place of friends' that special day. Someone had come to Camp wanting to volunteer. Bob, the new director, asked him to look for Curtis. He introduced himself to me as James Camp. I paused, thinking to myself, *"Did he say Camp?"*

I asked if he was ok with any type of work. James replied, *"I will do anything to help."* I responded, *"Ok, let's go to work ."* We started and would never stop. If we were not working, we would think about or talk about what needed to be accomplished. This was a new friend who spoke a language of details I understood. I know I said simple truths. James could do details simply. James wanted to work, and we did.

There is more to preparing for staff and campers than most friends may anticipate. Building and maintaining the site infrastructure while preserving the natural environment requires unique skills and an appreciation for simplicity. Balance is the lesson we learn and teach at Camp. Balance is the thing we can take with us wherever we may travel or call home.

What was it about James Camp? James had a respect for everything he would see, hear, or touch. The earth was life, and each living thing was tied together. We humans only played a small part. James had developed a special oneness with nature. James had a sense of community and responsibility to the natural world around us. James was attached emotionally to the mountains and everything in them.

That first day James and I met we were in our early twenties. We quickly became good friends. We would learn lessons we had not previously imagined. A desire to explore the future of a stronger community accessible to everyone in balance with the natural environment would be our guide.

We believed the experience at Camp could provide a perfect foundation for learning while having an exciting time outdoors. The program provided an opportunity for young people to participate in leadership training. Those young new leaders would help build the future. Together we would realize that future with new friends and growing families. Camp Unalayee was a "Place of Friends."

Were we really guided by simple truths or are these simply lofty words? We knew our elders place who came before us. Were we guided by our elders still attending their lessons? Over time my high school friend, Lowell, and I would grow old together along with James and countless others. We came to a place fortunate to look as far back as we could possibly see forward.

In this lifetime we became the elders. Together with our partners Jessie, Corinne, and Marianne we would know the early founders of Unalayee. Josephine, Margaret, Mary, Candice, Margot, Marsh, Paul and so many others had been our mentors and one day our elders. We would grow to know four generations of campers.

From their earliest memories our young families have always known Camp. In 1973, I would hike into Camp with little Corinne at just five weeks of age. One day Beth, Sarah, Becca, and Galen would each join us. They are now raising their families along with Phill, Cody, and Nick. Years later Little Corinne and I would hike into Camp carrying her daughter Sloane. Rose, Aria, Ruka, and Wilder would follow. There will be more to come as we had once imagined they would.

At Camp, while living together, a week can become timeless. A single session can feel like a unique lifetime. What guided this experience? Was it the natural environment or special friends? We were learning an important lesson. We recognized how valuable a guide would become.

These old friends would stay a good long while. I ask myself how we were guided by those simple truths. I believe the lessons of seven decades speak of something greater than lofty words and mission statements. As we look back and now forward, we have reached four of seven generations. I have learned something of what James knew and Lowell knows. What simple truths could we know? We would learn those lessons from our children's children.

12

FRIENDS LIKE NO OTHERS, PART 2, 1970'S AND BEYOND

CURTIS KOPPEL

Looking back on my early years, it was the 1950's when I was first introduced to the wilderness. I would not venture too far into the Bandelier, Cibola, Gila, or Sandia Wilderness without a guide. After those early adventures as a young scout, I became even more excited about exploring. Though unsure what path I might take, clues were beginning to mount. I was learning about what to avoid.

I was only 10 when each day of 4th grade I would walk Indian School Road near the base of the Sandia Mountains in New Mexico. I would look to the mountain top on my way imaging new adventures excited with what I might learn that day. I imagined I could one day explore every canyon and ridge top. After that year in 4th grade, I imagined I could do anything.

In 1970 my friend Lowell and I arrived at Camp Unalayee. We met our new friend, James Camp. We would become closer friends every year for decades to follow. James and I were working in Camp while Lowell was, again, on the trail. James and I imagined we could manage any job in Camp if we simply had the right tool. The trail, however, was calling us.

Alongside James, I was standing with a giant looking out at Bear Ridge. We were looking to the mountain top imagining what that day might bring. We could see Log Lake in the distance from where we were working. We began plotting how we could hike over to Log and back along the face of the ridge. Meanwhile, we had far too much to accomplish right there under our feet in Camp.

All the campers were out on trail hikes with all their counselors and Camp would be quiet that night. We knew friends would be camping at Log Lake. That evening James and I finished cleaning up after dinner with the small number of us left in Camp. Simultaneously we looked to the mountain top and back to each other. We could go up there now and be back before breakfast.

I knew there would not be a second to waste and no matter how quickly I could pack my sleeping bag, James would already be sitting at his rock with his bag packed along with our water and Swiss hikers' mix. He would be waiting for me. It was still early enough before dark with summer daylight. We took a high route, and, in a flash, we were on the face of Bear Ridge. I suggested we should scramble up to Butter Brick to have a look over the top, down to Bear Lake and out to the alps from the ridge. Only minutes later James may have saved my life.

Once we reached the top, we were now at the base of Butter Brick. I wanted to climb to the top. It was right there. James was clear that was not going to happen. I had a good-sized length of parachute cord in my bag to hang the Swiss hikers out of reach for the night. I could double or triple it up and he could surely save me if I slipped. *"No, we are not going to climb Butter Brick now and not with any parachute cord for a rope."* We had never argued, and never would, it turns out. I knew he was right even though I was certain we didn't really need a rope in the first place. Parachute cord was the wrong tool for the task. James was right on all counts. I was happy to be alive.

It was getting dark, but we could soon hear the friendly voices camped at the lake as we made our way down to Log Lake. We planned to leave at dawn. We would go down Horse Creek then up Tangle Blue Creek. We would stop only for water and Swiss Hikers' mix. In another flash we were back in Camp. James started preparing breakfast for the crew. I would run up to the lake and back before ringing the morning gong. James knew I checked the water at the lake every morning first thing. I have yet to miss a day in all these years since.

After breakfast we stood shoulder to shoulder, well as close as my shoulder could reach the tall shoulder of James. We were looking to the mountain top where we had just been. We knew then we could do anything. We would come to understand better just how much help we would need for the big jobs ahead.

Lowell, James, and I would dig ditches, form foundations, frame walls, and climb roof tops. Friday after working we headed to Yosemite to climb rocks. Meanwhile summers and Camp were never far away for Lowell and James. They lived for Camp and one day Fieldguides.

We raised families and journeyed forward. Our paths would join often. I was the lucky one. I had imagined I could do anything as I looked to the mountain top as a young explorer. Now I would travel with the best guides to the best places. I was with friends that would journey a lifetime together.

For years we would look to the mountain top and imagine we could do anything. My life well lived alongside Old Man Camp and Boss Man.

13

TWO MEMORIES, 1970'S
MELANIE JOHNSON

#1 We were waiting in the area where the buses came to pick up the campers. Campers and staff were saying their good-byes while the gear was loaded onto the buses. Lots of chatter and laughter. I noticed one camper - a boy - sitting off to himself. He was crying. I did not know him, but I approached him and asked if he was OK. He said he did not want to go home. We talked a little about what he had done in his time at Camp. I don't remember a lot about the conversation but do remember telling him he could come back next year. I will always wonder what was waiting for him at home and if he did return.

#2 WHEN I WAS WORKING, the campers went on two hikes during the two weeks they were at Camp. One hike with other campers and staff who were living in the same tribal unit. For the second hike the staff would lead different hikes and describe the hike and the campers would choose which hike they wanted to do.

Another female staff and I decided to do an "all girls" hike. I do not recall our destination or number of hikers or their ages BUT I vividly remember our last day. We approached Camp over the ridge by the Umbrella Tree. It is a long difficult almost straight up hike. Before beginning the trek up to the ridge we decided as a group to hike to the top without stopping - one step up at a time. My co-counselor led and I was at the end.

And we all did it - one step at a time - up to the Umbrella Tree. When we got to the top I think we were able to see Camp but I also believe that if anyone was in Camp they could hear us - lots of hooting and hugging. I know what it felt like for me to accomplish that trek up that ridge and am hoping that campers felt the same way and always wonder if - years later - they remember what it felt like.

BEING *part of Camp Unalayee changed my life. I was a staff member. I know for me climbing to the top of that ridge helped me complete 3 marathons, numerous half, as well as lots of shorter runs - then I biked up east coast, length of Mississippi River, across US, and down west coast - how it felt climbing to top of that ridge has never left me. Being a part of Camp Unalayee changed my life. Thank you for 75 years.*

14

THE FIRST UNALAYEE HIKING TRIBE, 1970

JOHN MARKOFF

My love affair with Camp Unalayee began in 1961 when I was 11, the first full year of Camp in the Trinity Alps. I was a camper and then a counselor-in-training, and in the summer of 1970 I returned to work as a counselor.

As a camper, getting to Unalayee had been an all-day affair. We had been bussed and then trucked in -- bouncing on top of our gear in a giant vehicle dubbed the UniMonster which arrived long after dark. By 1970, however, a new more direct road had been built to get from Scott Mountain summit to Camp and in June there was still light as I drove a VW bus up to a divide where a bit farther on you catch your first glimpse of Bear Ridge. I remembered Bear Ridge from hikes as a camper but soon after arriving at Camp, off to the West, I spied something else as well -- a distant range of snow-covered peaks.

These were the White Trinities, a pristine corner of the Trinity Alps Wilderness Area that feels more like the Sierra and less like the red-rocked, forested land that surrounds Unalayee. On the spot I made up my mind to hike there.

At the time the currency of the realm were the topographic maps that backpackers navigated by. You ordered them from the United States Geological Service, and at the time Xeroxing was barely a thing, so we lovingly cared for the maps and pored over them with the reverence of studying biblical texts. Mosquito Lake was located at the Northeast most corner of the Coffee Creek quadrangle. Probably at least 15 miles away by air -- in the farthest Southeast corner of the map -- were the White Trinities.

On the map I couldn't see the glaciers below Thompson peak, but the white granite surrounding Caribou Lake, reachable by a trail from a place called Big Flat, seemed completely straight forward and attainable. I traced a route from Umbrella Tree above Mosquito Lake to Wolford Cabin to the North Fork of Coffee Creek and then Coffee Creek Road to Big Flat.

How hard could it be I thought?

What I failed to reckon with were my brand-new leather hiking boots.

When I had been a camper, there had always been a tribe hike and a choice hike, three and four night trips respectively. Following a Swiss counselor by kicking steps up a snow bank with a number ten tin of apricots in my back will always be etched in my memory. I was certain that my backpack was going to pull me to my death.

In 1970 Bob Strickler had just become camp director and I persuaded him to create a new category for the first session choice hike called the "hiking tribe." We were given an extra day and with my co-leader Ginny Allen I recruited three campers: Johnny Ohta and Allen Edwards were older and experienced. We also took a younger camper, an outrageously smart and funny kid named Andy Van Borg.

We set out early, and if not for my blistered feet that had been tortured by a 10-mile slog along Coffee Creek, we would have made it. The trail down the North Fork past Hodges and Francis Cabin was easily among the best miles I've ever hiked. Precariously we crossed the creek on a giant fallen log at one point. We were overwhelmed by the intense vanilla scent of the Jeffrey Pines that are emblematic of the Trinities. Big Flat was in bloom with wildflowers that would just stop your heart.

Finally we gave up at the end of the day on what must have been the second or third night in a beautiful mountain meadow on the shoulder of Caribou Mountain, probably three or four miles short of our goal. I could hardly walk.

Getting back was brutal. We made it back to Big Flat and discovered Mountain Meadow Ranch, a dude ranch that several years later while on another hiking tribe I discovered offered an all-you-can-eat Sunday breakfast.

Five miles or so along Coffee Creek Road a guy in a pickup Camper truck took pity and offered us a ride all the way to Scott Mountain. My blisters were larger than 50 cent pieces on both heels and I quickly tossed all my Sierra Club principles out the window and accepted his offer.

Along the way we stopped at one of the U-turns on Highway 3 and dived into a pristine pool formed by the headwaters of the Trinity River. Years later when I returned, the rocks that rimmed the pool were covered with algae, but that summer that pool was as good as it gets for soaking my painful feet in ice cold water.

Late that afternoon he let us off at the top of Scott Mountain summit and the five us made our way -- in my case hobbling -- back to Camp.

I ATTENDED AS A CAMPER 1961-1964. I was a CIT in 64. I worked at Camp as a counselor in 70,72,76 and 77. I was on the board in the early '80s. I met my future wife, Leslie Terzian, at Camp in 1972. I'm a reporter and author. I've written five books including "Whole Earth: The Many Lives of Stewart Brand."

15

UNALAYEE'S TRUCKS 1970'S-2000'S
TOM BOUYE

In was hired in 1974 to keep the three old trucks running. That year, we barely made it to Gazelle before the electrical system went out and I had to replace the generator, the battery and the regulator.

In 1976 we got a Ford Crew cab stake bed. The tires were too small for the road, but it went on many memorable winter trips to the desert.

In 1988, we got a Chevy stake bed. It's still here running. It has 65,000 miles on it. It's perfect for the dozen trips to Scott mountain. It makes every year and stays in Shasta.

2001, we got a Ford pickup and put a big rack on it. It was our main vehicle until 2018, when we got The Beast. A true monster truck, and after seven years, it has 21,000 mi. They're hard miles.

I used to work on them. Now we tow them someplace; mostly to Tony's Dunsmuir Tire.

16

THE SWEAT LODGE, 1970'S-2010'S
JESSIE CAMP

For decades (1970s-2010s) the sweat lodge activity was a focal point for giving thanks to the land and the community it supported at Unalayee. Counselors and campers shared feelings and thoughts together during a facilitated ceremony filled with chants, songs, and spoken words. I was introduced to leading sweats by taking many led by Jim Wheeler during the summers we were both at Camp. In the 80's we held sweat lodge activities 3 times a session: Day 2, Special Day, and Day 14. In later decades, to save wood, we cut back offering the activity to just Special Day and Day 14. Sometimes the 10-day trail tribes would build sweats upon their return to Camp. Sweats happened regularly at Women's Week and Family Camp as well.

From setup to tear down, for me the whole process was like a ceremony of respect for the land and its gifts. It was always a labor of love.

During Opening or Staff Training, 2 or 3 counselors would build the sweat lodge using alder poles and canvas tarps. After checking on the alder poles' flexibility we would decide whether to harvest new poles that year. At the end of each summer during Closing, the poles were carefully laid next to the sweat lodge platform. By being buried under the snow all winter, they retained moisture and flexibility for several years. We later also put them in the lake for the same reason. If we needed new poles, a day hike ensued. Armed with hand saws, rope, and backpacks, we would go to an alder patch to cut about 10 poles from the plants. A prayer of thanks to the elements was given for the alder trees. Here's one of the songs I remember singing with Mike Wald on one foray:

"Thank you Mother Earth, Thank you Sister Water,
   Thank you for my birth, Thank you from your daughter.
   Thank you Father Sun, Sending Air in motion,
   Thank you everyone, Earth, Air, Sun, and Ocean."

We then hiked back to Camp with the poles tied to our packs.

Another half of a day was spent building the lodge. We used old canvas tarps (these were dried in the sun at Closing, before being folded up and carried to the craft shack for winter storage) to cover a domed frame made from the alder poles. It was simply done, using biffy shovels to dig holes for the poles and random cord to tie them all together. It was important to make the lodge sturdy, with ample headroom and space away from the hole dug for the hot rocks bucket, and to place and secure the tarps to allow no light to get in. The door always faced northeast to allow easy access to bring in the hot rocks from the large fire pit. We enjoyed engineering the space, crawling in and out to check for those elements and admiring the aesthetic of our work.

THE ROCKS. We gathered new ones every year because they would crumble from repeated intense heating over the summer. Our local peridotite (an extrusive igneous rock formed on the seafloor at crustal spreading zones) worked pretty well retaining heat. We would hike up to the ridge behind the sweat meadow to find and gather large enough rocks. It was also fun to hike up to the Washbasin Saddle and gather sage to tuck into the frame and also save for use during the sweats.

THE FIRE. We would dig out the fire pit each year and spread all the old coals into the woods. Before there was so much dead wood in Camp, firewood came from "wood runs" down the road. The Central campfire wood pile separated out "sweat wood" = the gnarly pieces that kids couldn't split. On the day of a sweat, anyone taking a sweat was asked to contribute by bringing wood from that pile. In the morning of a sweat day, the leader(s) would wheelbarrow those chunks up to the sweat and after building a fire with easier pieces, chop and use that wood for the all-day fire that burned.

There was a lot of prep and work-inspired reverence for the sweat lodge activity. But what was it like to take a sweat and what happened on the day(s) it was offered ?

At Morning Meeting, the afternoon activity was announced with an explanation of the intentions as well as the tangibles. Campers were invited to further their growing connection to the wilderness - that they had now lived in for a week or two - by joining in a ceremony of gratitude and respect for this place.

"Be sure to bring some 'sweat wood' and your own full water bottle with you." After hearing that taking a sweat meant enduring intense heat and darkness, it wasn't *everyone's* choice to attend, but nonetheless many kids seemed to like doing them year after year.

If you were at the waterfront during morning activities, you would hear the sound of wood chopping and see smoke rising from across the lake. A few counselors took turns tending the fire all day, and after Rest Hour you would hear a call of "SWEATS !" The gathering would begin. People arrived carrying wood, instruments, songs and crafts, perhaps ready to give massages or facials, or just wanting to quietly talk and hang out in the meadow with friends while waiting for a turn in the sweat.

It was fun to watch the sweat leader gather the hot rocks. This involved digging out a rock from the fire bed with a shovel, tossing it high in the air and catching it on the shovel blade to shake off small coals, and finally blowing off any remaining sparks before dropping it into the bucket. Two people would carry the bucket into the lodge using a specially notched stick. Meanwhile another bucket of sage-infused water was heating fireside. This simmering bucket was also carried in the same way, and placed in the back of the lodge where the sweat leader would sit. Hot stuff !

Some sweats were crowded, some were not, but regardless, everyone quietly lined up to listen to the leader's instructions and then crawled single-file into the lodge in a clockwise direction knowing that the back of the lodge was usually the hottest place, and being near the doorway the coolest. Once inside, the tarps were sealed tight and in the quiet darkness the smell of sage filled the hot air and the rocks glowed red-orange. *Hisssss...hissss*, a light steam rose from the rocks to welcome everyone in and sample the heat.

Every leader has a different style and approach to how words, chants, and songs are facilitated, as well as to how the heat is managed by pouring ladles of water on the hot rocks. Always, anyone can ask to leave at any time. Some folks like it hot and would rise to the ceiling and others like to stay down low and cool as possible. I enjoyed sharing so many wonderful songs, rounds, and chants learned over the years in that hot dark place together with friends who said many heartfelt, kind, appreciative, and grateful things to ancestors, family, friends in need, hard workers, other living species, and not forgetting the elements we depend on for our lives. As the rocks cool down, the sweat leader concludes the ceremony and someone pushes open the heavy layers of tarps and everyone crawls out, following around in the same clockwise direction. People often said, "All my relatives," upon leaving.

And afterwards, to the LAKE. How can I describe the feeling ?! Adjusting to the bright light, walking slowly, mud covered, sweaty, lowering into the muddied waters and invisible rocks, gliding out into a space in the lake, *those moments of floating, blessed be*.....climbing out, hugging friends, sitting or lying down next to them in the meadow, hearing the birds, "communing with nature," experiencing a pure "mountain high" in paradise. A golden afternoon. Feeling so very clean! Warming up in the sun or by the fire.

Soon, it's time for dinner and people help the leaders put out the fire with buckets and buckets of water from the lake. On Special Day we would usually arrive late, rosy and shiny-cheeked and hungry, feeling elated and grateful for (depending what decade you were there) some BBQ chicken and corn on the cob, or Lowell and James' red and green chili.

I'm not going to say that I think the sweat lodge was a "spiritual" center of Camp because I'm (still) not sure what that word really means, but I do know that humans who gathered together taking sweats on those afternoons felt love, and a deeper connection to each other and sometimes even to the complex web of life that is the Mosquito Lake basin. Afterall, we as humans evolved in wildernesses, as *a part of* complex ecosystems, and it's a good thing to remember that now and again.

CHRIS WILLIAMS HIRED *me in 1980. I went on Hiking Tribe to the Whites with Jim and Augie for my first session. From then on, I always tried to get out on the hiking or wild tribes, or a long choice hike. James Camp and I saw eye to eye on this, and we did many a trail tribe together over the years. Other Unalayee years' pursuits were: Program Director, CIT tribes, Women's Week, starting the Girls Getaway Trail Tribe, raising Galen and Sarah with James and the rest of the staff (Bless you all!!), Central work crew, work crew, work crew with Tom Buoye, holding (STILL!) the Umbrella Tree Run Women's record, leading HOT sweats, playing guitar with Tommy, teaching intricate seed-bead necklace making, leading singing and campfires at Family Camp, and seeing my daughter Sarah become Director and my son Galen partner Fieldguides with Unalayee. A great run of 44 years that continues, finding me now able to run around the basin with my granddaughters Rose Camp, and Rika James, Lee. I am grateful and I am blessed, thank you Unalayee.*

17

FIRST TIME I EVER, 1972
CAROLINE COOKE CARNEY

The first time I ever....
    slept outdoors under the stars,
owned a backpack,
hiked up and down a mountain,
battled hungry rats on a cliff,
sang at a Campfire,
made so many friends, and
planned meals, ordered food to over 250 campers and staff
...was at Camp Unalayee when I was 25.
    I also developed an appreciation for the Quakers who created a place for those of us who never had seen so many stars.

CAROLINE COOKE CARNEY was the Food Shack Lady in 1972. She is the Mother of Corinne Koppel and Sloane Birnbaum's Grandmother

18

SPIDERMAN'S WFA REFLECTIONS, AND OTHER MEMORIES AT CAMP UNALAYEE, PLACE OF FRIENDS, 1972-2024

TOM HALDERMAN, AKA SPIDERMAN

Over the past 52 years I have had many wonderful experiences and have made many great friends at Camp Unalayee, Place of Friends.

In 1972 I was a volunteer who was deeply affected by the core mission of Unalayee and the direct, indirect and other means by which that mission was (and is still) carried out by a staff of eclectic and dedicated souls. At Camp Unalayee, I saw a diverse gaggle of kids living in small groups in a challenging setting in the Mosquito Lake Basin and then go trekking throughout the Trinity Alps learning the meaning of self-reliance and fortitude through incredible hikes. Hikes to Marshy Lake, or to Grizzly Lake, Log, Bear, to the Reds, the Whites, the Marbles and myriad other inspiring and challenging adventures.

As a carpenter and builder, I have had many opportunities to repair and build structures at Camp. In 1983 I was asked to build a new tent platform by the Nurses' Shack as every tent platform in Camp had been mercilessly destroyed by an immense snow load the winter of 82-83. That platform by the Nurses' Shack still stands today. As we were a ridiculously poor organization back then, we did not use hardware to anchor the structure or to buttress its joints. Job built plywood gussets were utilized!

At the end of the summer of 1985, a small group of Unalayee leaders, including Lowell Fitch and James Camp, asked me if I would consider designing and building a new building (!!) which would be the office, storeroom and tool shed. The old wall tent that served as the office, mail room and spare gear room was worse than worn out and was woefully inadequate. Over the winter I designed the building and drew a set of plans, which were approved by the board of directors. Money was allocated and the summer of 1986 found me in Central with my truck and tools. (All hand tools, no power tools, no generator.) The plans were for a 16' x 16' building, which would be tucked out of the way so as to blend in with our environment. With the help of staff, work crew *and campers (!!)* we set to work. Miraculously, over the summer The **Chalet** was born! (It was named the Chalet years later after many a winter skiing sojourn utilized it as a cozy refuge in the snowy wintertime world of Camp Unalayee.)

As meaningful as constructing those buildings was, it didn't compare to what was next. In 1989 Lowell Fitch asked me to teach the wilderness first aid and rescue class as I had swapped my career as a builder for a career in emergency medicine.

In 1988 I became a paramedic. At 47 I graduated from UC Davis School of Medicine PA program and began practicing emergency medicine in the busy ER at Dominican Hospital in Santa Cruz. After a decade of that I moved to the Urgent Care Clinic at Santa Cruz Medical Clinic (which later became the Palo Alto Medical Foundation). I retired at 72 in 2017.

I HAVE TAUGHT wilderness first aid and rescue to the staff of Camp Unalayee, Place of Friends, almost every year since 1989. Teaching that class is one of the most profound ventures I have ever pursued. We laugh, we learn, we kid around and make bad jokes, and we have a blast.

It has been a privilege to work with our staff year after year! We build our personal and collective knowledge, with lots of lecturing, plenty of hands-on exercises, practicing near- drowning rescues, back board and Stokes basket carries, etc. We also explore all manner of traumatic injuries, infectious diseases and on and on. Environmental emergencies resulting from weather extremes are a major emphasis. My goal in teaching these classes is to share knowledge and insights that I have gleaned over the past several decades in emergency medicine with the Unalayee staff, our community.

I am dogmatic about respect. Respect for the campers' modesty, their agency, their space. Respect for who we are at Camp Unalayee, our history and our place in the world. And who we are, individually and collectively. We are a powerful force for good in the world.

There is a lot of humor and good-natured kidding involved with teaching that class year after year! I really am honored by the attention afforded to some of my expressions. Hey, who's counting? (Hahahahaha) BTW, "warsh yer hands!" How many times **did** I say: "Holy Toledo!!"? Where *is* weird Harold anyway?

Over the past fifty-two years I have watched Camp Unalayee grow from a ragtag, seat of the pants operation, barely holding its own, to a modern organization replete with a Campus loaded with modern amenities like cosmic composting biffies and more!

Thankfully, our core values and mission remain constant and as important as ever. We bring people from diverse backgrounds together, campers and staff. Our diversity is our strength. Our emphasis on dignity as an agency is our north star.

The most rewarding aspect of teaching the wilderness first aid and rescue classes over the past three and a half decades has been being fully immersed in our community and getting to know literally generations of counselors as friends and coworkers.

Camp Unalayee truly is the Place of Friends.

In 1972 I volunteered for work crew as suggested by my friends, James and Marilyn (Blue) Camp, and Dave McClellan. I've been on work crew ever since. I was on the board of directors in '80s and '90s and am now on the advisory board. I have worn many hats at Unalayee; always as a volunteer. I am a true believer in the mission and vision of Camp Unalayee, Place of Friends. The name says it all! "Place of Friends" is where it's at, Camp Unalayee!

19

HIKE TO RUSH CREEK LAKE, 1973
DAVE MCCLELLEN

Trinity County was special for its close connection with the past.
I was a counselor in '73. There is one recollection I would like to share: It is about a hike to Rush Creek Lake: We arrived at this seldomly used lake and found a recent camp that was made in an old-school woodsman's style: a table made of saplings nailed to a tree and a bed made of cut fir boughs with a sleeping bag set out.

Then up the trail comes an older (60?) gent with a pistol and a fishing rod and about 30 trout! He said he was a gold miner at Coffee Creek (and that he was from Germany, but lived in Coffee Creek part of the year) He said he was taking the fish back home to live on.

All of our group got a glimpse into the way of life in another time.

I WAS a counselor in '73+'74. I went on to spend a few years working for Outward Bound school in the Northwest. I still Backpack and Ski.(Although gravity seems to make things harder) I was a carpenter for 40 years and I live in Felton and am happily married. I have a son who went to Unalayee and also pursues outdoor pursuits w/ his family in New Mexico.

20

MY FIRST SUMMER AT UNALAYEE, 1974
FRED LIFTON

Note: This was the preface to my doctoral dissertation, something I never could have completed if not for the life lessons I gained at Camp.

WHEN I WAS eleven years old, I was sent away to summer camp. Like most young children undergoing this ritual, I was terrified at the prospect of leaving my home and parents for the unfathomably long period of two weeks. More terrifying still, however, was the fact that I was being sent to Camp Unalayee, a "wilderness camp" in California's Trinity Alps. Set deep in an alpine basin, Unalayee was without electricity, hot water or even permanent shelters. Instead of the usual mass of people, institutions and services that already encased my young life, my social world would contract to a total of twenty-five adults and about sixty-five children, all strangers. Instead of radio, television and sports facilities there was only a campfire circle, a lake and a tall-grass meadow. Everything I needed—heat, food, shelter—came directly from both my own and the labors of the fewer than one hundred people in the mountain basin.

Moreover, one of my two weeks there was to be spent backpacking; I would have to carry a pack over rugged country equipped with the bare minimum needed to survive, with only a handful of relative strangers for company. Instead of the familiar comforts of my bed and my room, I would sleep on the ground in a pine forest. For walls, I would have the steep, rocky ridges of an alpine lake basin. I hadn't done much in the woods during my short life, and I was a shy, skinny kid with a predilection for reading rather than rugged outdoorsmanship.

I made every effort to ensure I would hate these two weeks and to no small degree I succeeded. With a lot of hard work, I was able to make myself and, no doubt, my counselors quite miserable. And yet, when I got back on the bus after what felt like a geological age in the mountains, I was inexplicably sad to be leaving.

Today, I cannot say exactly what it was I had come to miss as a little boy. Perhaps it was simply the friends I had made, or the freedom from parental supervision, or my affectionate (and tolerant) counselors. Undoubtedly this new kind of social experience, neither school nor family, was liberating. But I can recall with surety that when I stepped off the bus the following summer and looked at the surrounding gray, rubbly peaks, when I heard the blue jays yammering and smelled the sharpness of the air and the pellucid sweetness of the pines, I knew that although I was only twelve years old, I had already fallen in love.

FRED IS A FORMER BOARD MEMBER, camper, CIT, counselor, and food shack goddess. He still serves on work crew as a volunteer every summer he can. His first counselors were Patsy Ohta and Dave Aquino.

21

JAMES AND THE BEAR, 1974

*As told by James Camp at campfire, 2017 or 2018,
recorded and transcribed by Matt Kohn*

This is a true story. It happened quite a while ago, I think it was in 1974, and it happened really close to here.

It's a bear story.

Now, we used to see bears more often in Camp. Back in '74, I must have been 28 or something like that, and Lowell (who many of you know, right?) and Corinne, and I, well, we took a hike. And we thought we were being really modern. Of course, now they have these getaway hikes where you're on the trail for 30 days. But back then we used to meet a group of kids right at the buses. It was already decided we were going to go on a hike with a wild tribe. And we'd meet them at the buses, and we'd hike for 14 nights. Then we'd end up coming back to the buses. So, we never even came here into Camp.

Now this is a story about a bear right at the end of a hike that we took.

We had just been out for 2 weeks, and our packs were pretty much empty. We were just coming in, below Camp a little ways, near the road, and I thought "I'm not gonna hike clear on down to the buses and carry my pack back up here. I'm just gonna set my pack down right next to this fallen log." And off we went.

Now, when I got back up to my pack, it wasn't leaning against the log any more. It was over on the ground. And I could see right away there was something wrong, because it was a faded old pack, but it had a bright patch on the front. That's where my map pocket had been, but it was just gone! But there was my map, right over there. The only thing of interest to anybody in my pack – I don't know why I still had it – was a single orange. And there was the orange, right next to the map. I realized it had to have been a bear that had just ripped that map pocket off, and found the one thing that it could possibly eat. So, I picked up the orange, and sure enough it had this hole in it, a little bit bigger than a pencil. I guess he'd just kind of stuck it with his canine tooth, said "Hmmmph, I don't like oranges," and dropped it and was gone.

And I was dumb, because there was my nice pack that I'd had for years. I loved that pack, and now I had to get a new one. Either that or repair it (which is what I eventually did). Well, I slung it over my shoulder and I walked up here to Camp.

Now, right about where that table is in Central – the one next to where the big tree's cut down – there used to be a tent platform. There were three or four people sitting on the deck in front of it, swinging their legs back and forth, making fun of the world, and laughing, so happy because they were going to get time off for a couple days before the next session started.

And I said "Look at my pack! A bear must have gotten to it, right down the road here a ways."

And they go "You hadn't heard?"

"Heard what?"

"There's been this bear in Camp, and it's been really a nuisance. A real problem for us. So we're going have a meeting in just a half an hour to decide what we're going to do with this bear."

Well, I was curious, so I went to the meeting, and the whole staff was there.

Now, this bear was acting very aggressively compared to most wild bears. Most wild bears, you see them and "whsht!," they're out of there like a shot. They're afraid of us because we're so dangerous, right? You know, we kill a lot of bears, and bears do us only a little bit of harm, mostly mess with our food. So, we talked about what we were going to do about this bear in Camp, because this bear was dangerous and seemed not to be afraid of people at all.

You know those green cabinets? That bear discovered that if he pounded on them really hard, the doors would fly open. And back in the 70's, we had a lot of what we called "big basics" in our tribes. For some of those basics, we had flour, and we had peanut butter, and we had raisins. These were in big glass jars. And a few other things, too. And the bear would just pound on this thing, because you know they just love peanut butter. He'd just break open a jar and start scarfing all this stuff.

People would come over and yell "Shoo! Shoo!" but this bear, unlike most wild bears, would just keep chugging down. He'd give them a mean look, and wouldn't budge an inch. He wasn't afraid of people, and that made people kind of worried. They started keeping all the food down in the food shack

And gradually all the tribes (or most of them, anyway) moved out to the lake. They were sleeping right along the edge of the lake because it was too spooky, especially up in Lake Camp. The trees are really thick there, and at night you don't want a bear sneaking up on you. Out at the lake you could see what was coming. So almost all the Camp, before the campers had even left on the last day, were camped out at the lake. And that's not a good place to camp because it gets really dewy every night. Everyone's sleeping bag would get damp, and they'd have to dry them out every day.

So, back to this meeting – what are we going to do with this bear? Seems like it's kind of dangerous having it around. Everyone's so scared.

Really, there were two groups. There was a group that was led by my friend Bill, and there was another group –I wasn't the leader, but I was one of the people in it – who had an opposite view. Bill's group said "Hey, listen. This is a really serious thing. We have a responsibility to these kids and to their parents. They expect us to be cautious in the extreme with their kids. We can't have an animal that's this big – it must weigh 150 pounds – that's not afraid of people. What if somebody stumbled on this bear and surprised it, and the bear attacked them and hurt them? That's happened in this part of the state."

And there was the other group, which I sympathized with. We said, "Oh, that's the wrong attitude. You know, listen, this is the wilderness area. And this bear, this is his home. Bears belong here. We can't go killing every animal that comes into Camp that inconveniences or scares us. You know, it's our fault. We let it get our food. We need to take better care of our food and better care of our garbage. Then we won't have a bear problem."

That was the basis of the argument.

Now, there were thirty-some-odd people at that meeting. And I don't know if you all have been to that many meetings, but everybody (and I was probably as guilty as the next guy), had to say their piece. And nobody said anything new after what I just told you. So, the meeting took about three-and-a-half hours.

And in the end, do you think we figured out what to do?
No.
Do you think anyone changed their mind?
No.
The only thing we could agree to was that we should get some help beyond our own experience. Somebody said, "There's a game warden who lives down in

Trinity Center." Trinity Center is about, oh, 30 miles from here. "Let's talk to him."

Bill and a few of the gang that thought this way got together, and a few people who thought like I did – I think there were eight of us altogether – well, we piled into this truck, and we drove down to Trinity Center. But, we didn't know where the game warden lived or where his office was. So, we pulled into the general store, and said "We hear there's a game warden here in town. Where's his office?"

"Oh, no, he doesn't have an office."

"Well, how do people get in touch with him?"

"Oh, go out to his place. It's at the end of Airport Road. Go out there, and it's the last house on the left."

So, we all jumped in the truck and drove out there. Going along, pretty soon seeing just a couple of shacks. Finally, there's this place at the very end of the road. And it looks like, well, I'll get in trouble, but I'll say it anyway, kind of like Appalachia. You know – a car lying around here and there, chickens running all over the place. Not too well kept up. And we thought we must have come to the wrong place, but we decided we'd go up and ask where the game warden is. So, we go up on the porch. Not all of us, but Bill and I and a couple other guys. And we knock on the door (on the screen door because the other door is already open). Bang, bang, bang, bang!

No answer.

Bang, bang!

Well, maybe nobody's there.

We just start to leave when we heard some noises – knocks – from inside the building. Well, somebody's in there. BANG, BANG, BANG, again. And, finally, this guy comes up to the door. He's on the other side of the screen door.

"Yeah, what?"

Now this guy is like, seedy, right? We're all thinking "We're in the *wrong* neighborhood. Must have hit a bad turn." But we just say, "We're trying to find the game warden."

He kind of looks at us like…well I won't say what I was gonna say, because it's a four-letter word which I shouldn't mention. Well "blank," but plural. That's how he's looking, but he doesn't say it. Finally, he says "Yeah, I'm the game warden."

"Oh, well, we're from that Camp Unalayee."

You could just see him shaking his head. I don't know if he'd heard anything about Unalayee, but he was clearly thinking "Why are these guys coming here bothering me?"

We didn't want to tell a long story because he wasn't interested. That's what it seemed like, anyway. So, we tell him about this bear and that we're worried about it. And all the time, he's just shaking his head like "What are you down here bothering me for?" A pretty unkempt guy. He was kind of skeptical of things, you know.

He says "OK, listen – here's what you can do. You shouldn't have let him get your food and garbage, you know?" OK, we realize that... "You ever thought of trapping him?"

Everybody kind of perks up their ears. "Trapping him?"

"It's not easy, but you want to try?"

We're all nodding our heads "Yeah, man."

"OK. Bring your truck around back."

We back the pickup around back of his house. And he goes over to this thing, and it's a bear trap. I don't know if you all have ever seen a bear trap. You're probably picturing one of these big steel spring things that "Chh-hhrapp!" gets their leg, right? Because there are traps like that. But those are illegal here, and we didn't use those, even back in 1974. But this trap, it's big. It's like a big metal culvert. It must be 3 or 4 feet in diameter and about 8 feet long. One end's got this screen welded on it to close it off. And in the other end there's this big door that slides up on runners, and it's got this big heavy-duty spring welded into it. The door kind of rises up and clicks into place. And the trick is there's a little trigger right down here at the closed end. So, the bear's got to come in from the open end, and if it touches this trigger near the closed end, it causes the screen door to fall down, like a big guillotine. Right?

He shows us this thing. We say, "Tell us how this works."

He says, "Well, you go into the trap. You put something – anything – the bear will like on that trigger. Then you set the trap somewhere where the bear's been active, and hope for the best. Right?" And he adds, "Yeah, it doesn't always work. Sometimes they won't go in."

So, we're all going "Yeah!" and we load this trap into the back of the truck.

We're just getting ready to go, and he says "But, wait a second. It's really hard to catch these bears. You know, you might have to shoot him."

And all of a sudden you could see Bill's eyes light up and his ears perk up, because that's what he'd been saying all along – we've gotta kill this bear, or get someone professional to come in, so he's gone by the time the campers come. And here's the game warden saying "You may have to kill this bear."

Now the rest of us were thinking "*Us*, kill him?" But Bill was smiling and kind of nodding his head. And there were no words said, but the game warden looked straight at Bill and said "You know how to handle a gun, right?" We hadn't talked about any of that, but Bill goes "Yeah," because he'd been in the army ROTC in college, and they had done rifle training and marksmanship and all that. So, he knew how to handle a gun, although he'd never shot a big animal.

Then the game warden goes "Wait a second," and goes back in his house and we hear him rumbling around in his bedroom – we could see it through the screen door. And he comes out with this thirty-aught-six hunting rifle [thirty caliber Winchester rifle]. And he looks straight at Bill and says, "OK. If you have to shoot him, I'm going to write you out a permit, and you can shoot him. You know, you may not be able to trap him."

Bill says, "OK. Yeah." And you could see Bill was pretty stoked about this.

But we were trapping this bear, right? So, we drive back up to Camp with our trap, and with our gun on loan, and with this permit to shoot what they called a nuisance bear. And we actually drove right up in past the wood pile, a little farther on. And you know where that really big tree is? Right on the other side of that big tree, right there, we put that trap out. Because we figured that was one of the paths this bear was taking. There was lots of bear poop. And man, that bear poop was amazing, too. We'd look at it, and remember how I told you he'd been knocking these jars out of the cabinets, right? With the peanut butter and the raisins and stuff? There were these big old chunks of glass. Because I guess they got such a strong stomach or something, he'd just pass them right on through.

So, we put the trap up and we said "OK, we gotta put something on the trigger. What's it gonna be?" And we decide that we'll put a combination of things on it. We'll put some peanut butter, because he's been eating peanut butter the whole time. And we'll sweeten the pot with some sardines because that's fishy smell, right? And he'll like that.

Now, somebody had to go into the trap, right? Guess who? Yeah, it was me! It's a disadvantage sometimes to be large. But I had to go into this trap, and remember I'm only 28. I can't do it anymore, I can't even demonstrate hardly. But you gotta bend way down to get into this trap and you go on back.

But the trouble is, what happens when a bear is trapped? The same thing always happens. The bear gets scared. And they poop and they pee all over the place. So, the whole inside of this trap smells like that four-letter word again. It's really bad. Yeah, exactly, it's all over the sides of this thing. Why they don't sterilize or clean it out, I don't know, but they don't. So, I'm back in there – "Oh, gosh, got a little on my shirt!" you know? "Oh, got some on my back!" Anyway, I get back to the trigger, and I put that peanut butter and that sardine on the trigger, and "Oh, got some on my pants!" And finally I get out of the trap. Well, I was glad to get out!

And everybody was kind of relieved, you know? It's getting a little late, starting to get dark. And we think, "Oh, yeah, gonna be a moon out tonight. Bears are active when the moon's out especially. And he's been coming by here all the time. We can see by his poop, it's all over the place over there. Maybe he'll be interested. Maybe we'll catch him."

And so, everybody was going out to the lake. Probably all but 6 or 7 counselors. And I was like "Oh, come on you guys. It's a California black bear. It's not a grizzly bear. There have been so few killings from black bears." I mean, it happens, but it's rare.

"And this bear's interested in food, he's not interested in me. I'm gonna sleep up at my spot," which was up by Lake 3.

Well, I went up there, but I was giving them a hard time, all those guys at the lake. "Ah you guys, such scaredy cats, you guys are so chicken." We had fun ripping each other. There were still a few people – Lowell and Corinne were still sleeping out there. Carmen was still out there. And a couple other people. But most everybody was out at the lake.

And so, I'm going up to my spot, and no sign of any bear. I didn't hear any bears. I had a lantern with me in addition to my flashlight. That lantern was lit, and I was reading a book by Farley Mowat. *Never Cry Wolf*, that's the name of it. It's about this guy up the Arctic who studies wolves, and he learns a lot about them. I was reading that book for maybe half an hour before I went to bed and turned off the lantern. I used to sleep really good back then. And I know half of you all do, too.

All of a sudden, in the middle of the night, it's like you're sleeping and then you're totally awake and you hear something in your brother's room down the hall. You can just hear it so clearly. And that's just the way it was. I was asleep one second and totally alert the next, because I could hear little twigs breaking. I was out under the stars, and it was coming from back in that direction. And I knew right away it was a bear. And I was scared. So, I sat straight up, and you never saw anybody light a lantern faster, right? I got that thing going in, like, 15 seconds! Then I could see really far because those old gas lanterns were really powerful. But, do you think I could see the bear? No. Because a bear, if it wants to be quiet, you can't hear it. They're so stealthy.

So, I looked all around. I got up and walked around. I'm thinking, "Darn, now I'm kind of freaked out. But I can't very well go down to the lake because I've been giving them a bad time. I'll never hear the end of it. What am I gonna do?" And then I thought, I'd just been reading that book, right? By Farley Mowat about the wolves? In there, he describes how the wolves are very territorial, and they mark the boundaries of their territory, which can be miles around, by peeing around the border of their territory.

I thought, "Yeah, maybe this works with a bear, too." So, I started that night. I kind of figured, "OK, this is going to be my territory. I'll just pee here, right now. Then maybe I'll get up once in the night, and I'll pee over there. And I'll pee over there in the morning." I thought, "The bear will smell my urine, and he will respect my territory. This is my place, not his." So, now I'm going to sleep.

Not everybody was asleep that night because two of the younger staff members, Victor and Johnny – I think they were 18 at the time– they decided they would go down and they would hide in these bushes over here. They could see down into the trees where the trap was. If they saw the bear, well, that would be cool, right? You'd like to see a bear get trapped, that would be neat. And so, they're there.

Sure enough, they said about one o'clock in the morning, the bear comes up. They could see him walking perfectly. He looks in. They could tell he's smelling, thinking "Mmmmm...I smell something good in there." But, he must have also smelled that scared bear smell. You know, all that poop, and that pee, and who knows what all else bears give off when they're totally distraught. And so, he wouldn't get in it. He'd walk around it. And finally, to add insult to injury, that bear crawls up and sits on top of the trap.

Now, when you're 18, it's really hard to resist when you're snubbed like that, and it seems like you can't do anything. But of course you *can* always do something. They said to each other, "Hey, let's lob some big old rocks down on this bear." Now these are strong young guys. They can throw a rock pretty hard. So they start launching missiles. The bear looks at them, and he doesn't like it, having rocks thrown at him, so he takes off after them!

Fortunately, they weren't that far below the craft shack...it's not the same craft shack there now, but it was in the same place, and it was this steep A-frame with that 60° angle. It had one of those green tarpaper roofs on it with those really rough rocks in the tar paper. Well, they got to this thing, and they were so scared, with their adrenaline going, they managed to climb that tarpaper roof, right up to the pitch. So now they're a little under 15 feet off the ground.

Well, the bear comes steaming up. And it was such a dumb thing for them to do because bears can climb. Well, grizzlies can't climb at all, but I've seen black bears climb trees a lot. They could race right up this tall tree in just a couple seconds. And they wouldn't even need branches, they're that good at climbing. So that bear could have climbed right up that craft shack. But for some reason he didn't. He stopped there, and Victor and Johnny, they're stuck on the top of roof looking down at the bear.

I guess he stayed there for over an hour, looking around, walking around. And they're just like "Ohhhhhhh........." Right? And then, he leaves.

They stayed up there for about another hour. And then, finally, they got brave enough, and they came down, and they ran to the lake. And then, of course, it was a big story. "This is a killer bear! It tried to chase us, it would've eaten us alive, yada yada yada."

So, we didn't catch the bear.

Bill says "Well, we tried. Gotta shoot him now." "Whoah, whoah, whoah!" says the others.

So, we had another meeting.

That meeting had almost the same people in it. And almost the same arguments. Except now it was a killer bear, right? And, again, it lasted 3 or 4 hours. We started early in the morning. Do you think anybody changed their minds? No. Do you think anybody refused to comment? No. It was terrible. But the only thing we could agree on is that we'll go down and talk to the game warden again. Tell him what happened, and see if he has any suggestions. The bear wouldn't go in the trap.

There weren't as many as the day before, but Bill was still there, and I was still there, and a couple other people, and we drove the truck down. We drove up in front of the game warden's house. He was sitting in an old run-down chair on his porch. You could just tell he thought we were so stupid.

We told him what had happened.

He didn't say many words. He said "Well, I told you it wasn't likely... ah! There's one thing you can try." He said, "Now don't you tell anybody about this, but I'm going to tell you. This is a secret. You know, there's one thing that bears find very hard to resist, and you might try it to trap him tomorrow or tonight." He said, "Take a little honey and burn it, so it'll have a smell. Put that on the trigger and see what happens."

The reason you want to do this is, well, everybody knows bears love wild honey. But the problem is bears don't get it very often without a lot of pain and suffering. We think they're covered with all this heavy fur. And they are, and that protects their bodies from bee stings. But when they find a hive, they'll start tearing into it, despite the pain of getting stung on their lips, and their nose, and their tongue. All that's vulnerable to bees, and it hurts them a lot. But, if there's been a forest fire, the heat kills the bees, and it scorches the honey. Somehow, over the millennia, bears have learned that when you smell the burnt honey, bees are dead. So, you can go straight to the honey because you don't have to worry about getting stung when you're tearing the hives apart. And so, apparently, they can't resist it.

We go "OK, the kids are coming. We gotta get him tonight." Because at the meeting, we agreed, well, if the ranger can't get him, Bill gets to shoot him if he can find him. Maybe he'll stay down by the trap, or whatever. So, we're all really crossing our fingers.

We drove back up, and put some honey in a pot on the stove. Sort of smelled like caramel at first. I didn't even like the smell. And believe me, I wasn't the one who crawled into the trap, somebody else did. He got a bunch of it on him, too. He put burnt honey on the trigger and came out.

It was getting dark by the time we did that. Bill comes up to me and he says, "You looked at that trap?"

I said, "Yeah."

"You know, that bear can get out of that trap."

"What? No, that's a bear trap."

But Bill was a lot smarter than I was. You all know what Mensa is? It's a society of people who have a tested IQ of 140 or more. Technically, they're geniuses. And Bill was one of those. He was much faster than me and could think of things. He said, "Yeah. I've been looking at that trap. That bear can get out of there."

"Bill, that's a bear trap. It's meant to keep the bear in. It's not gonna let him out."

"Well look at this. Come on over here. Look at this track that the door runs on. Do you notice if we put this door down, these pin holes on both sides line up. What do you think that's for?"

"I don't know."

"That's to keep the bear from turning around in the trap and putting his claws in that metal welded-on wire, and lifting that thing up and getting out. Couldn't you do it if you were inside?"

"Well, yeah, but I'm not a bear. I'm more like a monkey, right? We've got some thoughts that bears don't have."

"Well, I think the bear could lift it up and get out."

"OK. OK. I don't want you to shoot the bear, whatever you think. So what are you getting around to?"

"Well, let's sleep down here, up the hill in the trees. Not where we can see the trap, but where we can hear what's happening. And, if the bear gets trapped, I'll take the thirty-aught-six and cover you while you go down and slip a big bolt through those holes when they line up."

See, he was smart. I was the one who had to go down and maybe get chased, while Bill was up there with the gun and was supposed to shoot him if he tried to chase me.

I wasn't scared, I didn't think the bear could get out, so I said "OK, whatever you want, as long as we don't shoot the bear. I'll go get my stuff."

So, I started up. It wasn't dark yet, just getting dark. The moon was already out. And I'm going up, and I'd just gotten to about where Lake 1 is, and I start to hear this strange noise. Right away, I started to get goose bumps, because I knew what it was. It was this scraping sound. And what that is, well bears like to drag their claws in the bark of trees. It sharpens their claws. And there was a bear, somewhere back there towards Lake 3, where I was camped, making this sound.

And I went "Mmmmm Hmmmm..." You know how sometimes you just go "OK, you can do this James," right? "Go on ahead and get your sleeping bag. I know you're scared, just keep going, though." And so I kept going a little ways.

And then I came to Carmen's spot, which was before mine, and it was just scattered everywhere. So I guess he'd been up in Lake Camp for a while before I got there. And I got a little farther, and I came to my spot. Same thing. Everything scattered all over the place. I'd been sleeping under the stars, and there's my sleeping bag laid out. And do you think the bear was trying to tell me something? About territory? There was this huge pool of bear pee sitting right in the nylon of my sleeping bag. And for a moment, I wanted to kill the bear, too!

By the way, never let a bear pee on your sleeping bag because you can't get the smell out. I brought it down, and I washed it a gazillion times. But that night I went down to the campership sleeping bags, and I got one. Then I went up to the tent platform that Bill and I were going to sleep on that night.

I thought I'd be up all night, you know, not able to sleep. But I went to sleep pretty fast. And then it just seemed like a few moments that I was asleep, when BAM!!! We heard this trap door come down. And of course that meant the bear had triggered the trap, and he was probably inside.

We got dressed really fast. It wasn't until it was all over that I realized I had my tennies on the wrong feet. We came down here, and Bill's standing back, but not real far. He's got his gun kinda pointed at the ground. I went up, and I had this bolt that I stuck right through there so the bear couldn't get out.

And the bear was in there. It was really amazing. He hadn't even turned around. But I will never forget the sound the bear was making. I can't quite make it for you, but it was a sobbing sound. I thought he was crying. Now Tom Marquette – some of you know him, right? – he became a wildlife biologist over at Redwoods National Park. He tells me, "You know, it's more likely he was really angry. That's the sound they make sometimes when they're really angry."

Maybe. I didn't know. I thought he was crying. But whatever he was doing, it really hit me right here in the heart. Wow, here's this animal who has feelings, and we've scared the – there's that word again – out of him. It really hit me, you know?

Anyway, I went "Shhhhheeeeeshhh. Glad that's over with. Let's go back to sleep."

And Bill looks at me and, because he was smarter than me, he says "We can't do that."

"*What?!*"

"Yeah. Look at where this trap is. It's going to be in the full sun, shortly after sunrise. That bear, he can't take that heat. We've gotta send somebody down, right now, to the game warden's house so he can come up early in the morning and tell us what to do, now that we've got this bear."

So, we went out to the lake, sure enough. OK, who wants to go to town? You know, 18 year-old boys want to have an adventure. Johnny and Victor: "Yeah! We'll go!" So, they jumped in the truck. It's like 4 in the morning. And they went down.

Next morning, sure enough, the sun came up. And it wasn't long before we heard the trucks coming up the road. Our truck first and, right behind them, the game warden.

The game warden, well, this was the first time I saw him smile. He was kind of chuckling. "Oh, yeah, you caught that bear. You know, there's a lotta bears here. We've been studying the bears. They're interesting. You want to help us do a few things?"

"Like what?"

"Well, we'll take him out of there…"

"*What?!* We'll take him out of there? We just got him *IN* there!"

"Oh, no, no, no, no. This is going to be really safe because we're going to tranquilize him before we take him out."

The game warden, he's got on this really grubby old military surplus jacket with the big pockets. And he reaches into one pocket. "Yeah, we're going to tranquilize him. This is sodium pentothal, so we can take him out of the trap and make a few measurements"

And we go, "Mmmmmm…are you sure about this?"

"Oh yeah, we do it all the time."

So, he got this needle, and we realized that in this trap, there were all these slots in the wall of that corrugated culvert, about an inch-and-a-half long and half an inch wide. And the idea is, you can stick a needle through there and give the bear a shot of this sodium pentothal, which would just knock him out.

But you know, the bear was really smart. We'd go around to where his butt was, but he'd move his butt right away. And we couldn't get him. So, the game warden – you know how he looked at Bill when he gave him the gun, but this time he looked at me. And he said, "You know, I didn't tell you this. There's one other thing that bears can't resist [and now I'm gonna tell you that, too], and that's Smucker's strawberry jam."

And he reaches into the pocket on this side of his jacket, and he pulls out this jar. Well, there pieces of twigs and stuff stuck to the side of it, but he takes off the top, and he fishes a stick like this off the ground, and he gets a bunch of that strawberry jam on the end of the stick. He put the cap back on and puts the jar back in his pocket. It was all sticky and gross, but he did it anyway.

And he said "Here, you put this over by those holes at the front of the cage, and see what happens."

Sure enough, I put this thing right by one of those little holes, and the bear went straight over there, and he's trying to lick it. Right? He didn't even think about his butt. His butt came right up beside some holes at the other end of the cage. And the game warden just reached over and went Whhshht! and gave him the shot. I guess the bear couldn't resist the Smucker's strawberry jam.

It wasn't long, maybe a minute or so. First, he just started to kind of like sway a little bit, and then he just "skonk!" curled up on his side and went to sleep. Just from one shot. "OK! Let's take him out!"

"Are you suuuuure?"

But we pulled up that door. It was Tom Marquette and I. And we pulled this bear out. Now this bear, he's been in there, just like every other bear, and he's pooped and peed all over the place. So, his fur has got – there's that four-letter word again! – all over himself. And we pulled him out, and we put him in our laps. We didn't even care that he was covered in his own poop and stuff. I mean, he was in our laps!

And that game warden would say, "OK, take this measure." It was one of those cloth tapes. "And tell me how big it is around his thigh." And we'd measure that. Then he'd say, "How about his forearm?" or whatever. And we'd measure that.

His bicep was bigger than our thighs!

The warden measured his neck, and he opened up his mouth, and he could tell by looking at his teeth how old he is. "Oh, this is a pretty young bear. He's only about 3 years old. Let's weigh him."

Well, he had this sling, and we kind of inched the bear in there against a tree. Then we'd lift him up a little, and he weighed just under 300 pounds. And the warden says "No normal bear ever gets to be 300 pounds in three years. This bear has been eating human food for a long time. And that's why he's not afraid of you, because he's used to people."

Then he said, "Well, let's put him back in that trap."

And we did, and he covered it with a tarp, and he drove him off, he later said a hundred miles away. And we all patted ourselves on the back, and said "Oh good, we got rid of our bear."

But later, when Tom was a wildlife biologist, he found out the truth about that. The warden did take him a hundred miles away, but the chance that he'd live was small. Because, just like you, if they took you to the center of some new place and dropped you off. Someplace like that. You wouldn't know what to do, you wouldn't know the people. They might not treat you right. And the same is true with the bear. You drop him off a hundred miles away in some other bear's territory, and he's already been given sodium pentothal earlier in the day, so he's kind of groggy. Maybe he'll try to cross the highway to get back to his home. So, a very small percentage of bears live after they've been through all that. That's what Tom said.

So, anyway, the bear was gone, and we didn't have a problem. But, you know, I remember to this day, even though maybe I had the emotion wrong, I know he had some feelings. And when I heard that sound I thought was crying, it touched me here. It made me feel close to a wild animal.

Thanks for recording and transcribing this story, Matt!

22

LANTERN MAN, 1975
TOM MARQUETTE

There was a time when liquid gas powered lanterns were the optimum way to make a bright light in the forest. They were messy, noisy and dangerous. They produced a harsh white light and a unique and disturbing sound that didn't fit in with Camp's peaceful surroundings.

This was the case in the summer of 1975.

In those days during choice hikes, almost everyone in the Camp Unalayee basin would be out on a hike or a day off. During this particular week, I stayed back as the truck driver/EMT in case someone needed to be rescued. I was accompanied by a second staff member, Sutie Lewis, who stayed due to a medical issue, but was now ready to enjoy the peace and solitude of an empty camp.

The night of the sighting was warm, with a small breeze and except for a few clouds rolling by. At this elevation the night sky was a blanket of stars and with no city lights or coastal haze in a way where you could almost touch them.

After dinner and a bit of small talk in Central with Sutie, I decided to hit the hay. My eyes adjusted to the darkness quickly, so no flashlight was necessary. I passed Sutie's sleeping spot in some trees next to the trail above the lake that went just below the last Lake Camp.

Here, there was a clearing containing a make-shift kitchen with a cooking fire grill, food prep tables and storage cabinets that a group of campers called home when they were in Camp.

From there I took a small but all too familiar trail that wandered down through the forest for about forty yards where it passed my sleeping spot. This was nothing but a small almost level patch of ground with just room enough for a small backpacking tent with a door that faced back up towards the group camp.

From here I could see the stars straight above me and back up the trail, the tops of the trees that bordered the kitchen clearing. Watching small clouds drift past the treetops, I fell asleep.

My sleep was disrupted by something I couldn't completely put my finger on. Looking up the trail I could see that the tops of trees around the camp site were illuminated from below. It looked like the light from a gas lantern. Thinking someone may have returned from their hike due to a possible emergency, I got up and made my way toward the light. When I was close enough to almost see the source, I realized that there was no lantern sound. In fact there were no sounds at all. In another couple steps I figured I'd see what was going on. Then all of a sudden, the light went out. The only illumination at all was from the stars.

I walked into the opening of trees and the camp site. Nothing looked disturbed. Thinking that things weren't making sense I searched around a little and found nothing. I leaned against a table and just listened for a minute but couldn't hear anything but the quiet of the forest. Perplexed, I returned to my sleeping spot. As I arrived, I looked over my shoulder toward the camp. The trees were again lit up from below.

This time I quietly and cautiously approach the trees at the edge of the clearing. As if to surprise the light, I jumped out from behind the trees where the forest met the clearing. This time I again surprised myself. No light and no sound, just the haunting feeling that I was being watched. As I made my way back to my tent, I noticed the wind had picked up and was blowing thin clouds around. More than once I resisted the urge to look back until I was at my sleeping bag. I turned my head and again saw the trees were lit up by the strange glow. Once in my bag, my eyelids gave up and I lost sight of the harsh unnatural light that continued to shine in the forest.

The next time my eyes opened the morning sun had taken over. Birds were singing and warmer morning air pulled me out of my sleeping bag. As I walked down to Central through the camp sites, I noticed that everything looked normal and undisturbed.

I could smell coffee and heard Sutie moving around in the kitchen. This got me thinking of how or if I was going to tell her about the strange light. Maybe it had all been a dream, With a smile and a good morning I was handed a steaming cup of coffee. A feeling of normalcy was beginning to wash over me until Sutie asked, "What were you doing last night walking around at all hours with that damn lantern?"

The hair on the back of my neck was now standing up. I asked what she meant. She went on to say that she saw a light hanging out in the campsite above her spot that eventually wandered down the trail close to her. I asked if she had actually seen a person or heard anything like footsteps or the hiss of a gas lantern.

Her answer was no, and her face looked perplexed. I told her of my experience that night and that it wasn't me she had seen. After a very long pause we discussed every logical scenario we could think of that explained the light.

As these panned out, one by one, we then began discussing the illogical explanations. Even though the scientist in me was having a hard time grasping the supernatural implications, we couldn't deny that the strange bright light had us perplexed.

Let's just say, sleep didn't come easy for the next few nights.

As the years have passed others have reported seeing an unexplainable light in the trees. One would be wise to look over their shoulder now and then when walking through camp in the dark of night.

I worked full summers at Camp for 7 years starting 1971. I've been a counselor, lifeguard, truck driver and first aid instructor. In 1979 I started working full time at Redwood National Park, and worked there for 34 years. I volunteered as the Camp Nurse for many years. I am currently retired.

23

RATTLESNAKES, 1975
CHRIS WILLIAMS

It was my first season (first session) at Unalayee and Tom Buoye was my co on a hiking tribe. We were dropped off at Lover's Camp trailhead with 8 excitable campers ready for the long hike back to Camp.

Within the first couple of days we faced our first challenge: a camper experiencing an emotional crisis. Tom and I decided to hike our group to the nearest trailhead and evacuate our camper. A 20-mile hike lay in front of us, difficult even in the best of circumstances.

Morning progress was good and after our lunch stop at an old cabin we resumed our hike. I was in the lead and within the first 100 yards the camper just behind me yelled "rattlesnake." We immediately stopped and observed a very small rattlesnake trying to hide under a rock adjacent to the trail. Cool.

After a cautious examination, we headed back down the trail. No more than 50 feet further and I immediately froze at the sound of dozens of agitated rattlers warning me. A rattlesnake den just feet from the trail! This den was on top of a large pile of rocks to my left and a steep wall on my right. No easy way around.

Tom, at the back, was impatiently inquiring why we had stopped. He and most of the group could not see or hear what I was stopping for. I remember saying "Just back up" as I gingerly edged away from the snakes.

After much discussion and consternation we decided the only option was to throw a rock into the middle of the snakes and then hurriedly go by. Well, the snakes did scatter among the rocks and now, unfortunately, we couldn't see where they were. So, brandishing my trusty hiking stick I stood guard as the group passed by hoping my exposed ankles didn't turn into an appealing destination for snake fangs.

The rest of the hike was long and hot, but we got to our destination, Idlewild Campground. Tom hitchhiked back to Camp hoping to return the next day to evacuate our camper. Myself and the rest of our group slept soundly that night only to be awakened next morning to the excited sounds of Keith Vandevere, a camper returning from the bathroom, warning us about a large snake heading directly towards our campsite of still sleeping folks.

Hopping up I grabbed my trusty stick and carefully, with immense concentration, removed the confused reptile to a better place.

And so began my long association with Camp Unalayee.

CHRIS WILLIAM WAS *on staff from 1975 to 1985 (1979 and 1980 director), intermittent work crew volunteer 1987 to 2019, and is currently semi-retired, and still backpacking .*

24

FIRST SUMMER, 1977
WALTER CHUCK

My mom was looking for a new camp for me to go to for the Summer of '77. She was looking through *Sunset Magazine* and saw an ad for Camp Unalayee, a wilderness camp in the Trinity Alps. Mom had me call the office and talk to the lady in the office (Claudia?). She was really nice and encouraged me to go. I asked the office to send the information to us, Mom signed me up for 3rd Session that year. We went down the gear list and got most of the things on it.

The drive to Cubberley HS was early, but I was excited to get on the bus and go. The guy I rode next to was a "Jake," too, and we talked about what might be in store for us. The bus ride was long, but the drive up the Camp road to the turnaround was exciting. I am still amazed that they used to do this. I met my counselors Mark and Ginny and the rest of my tribe at the turnaround. We hiked into Camp and got all the tribe's gear up to Lake 2.

I liked Camp right away and enjoyed walking around the lake, archery, fishing and campfire. We were one of the younger tribes, our tribe hike was to the EBPs and Ringers cabin. I had been hiking before but never backpacking, it was not as easy as I had thought but I made it back to Camp.

When choice hikes were announced almost all of them were going to be mostly cold food due to fires. One was going to be able to have hot food, so I chose that one; Bear, Little Bear and Log Lake, probably not the best choice for a 10-year-old new hiker. The hike to Bear was long and going down the chute the first time was a little scary but fun. We made it to the Campsite, it started to rain as we set up and it did not stop for 2 days.

The leaders brought us our meals, checked up on me and my tent mate and made sure we stayed as dry as possible. My stuff was pretty wet by the time we packed up to go. The hike back was not fun, I was cold, wet, tired, my pack was full of wet stuff and heavy. I started to lag behind, most of the group went ahead. My tent mate and one of the leaders, Beth, stayed with me and encouraged me to keep going. The sun started going down, I was pretty much done, so we set up Beth's tent. The three of us had trail mix and Zing for dinner.

The three of us were woken up by loud creaking and bouncing headlights and soon after by flashlights and voices. Tom, Lowell and James had driven down to the Tangle Blue road in Beulah to check on us. They brought us dry sleeping bags and asked if we wanted a ride back. "No, we are OK and will see you back at Camp," the dry bag was very welcome and sleep came very quick.

We woke up to a sunny morning packed up and started back. When we got near Camp some people saw us walking up, they came down to ask how we were, glad you made it back, and good job for finishing the hike. Those simple gestures that night and morning meant a lot to that little kid and taught him about himself and the kindness of others. The last days of Camp went by pretty fast. I was ready to go home, sad to leave and eager to return. My choice hike the next year was Bear, Little Bear and Log. The years I was at Unalayee went by too fast but what I learned from others and about myself have never left me and I have hopefully passed them on to others.

Unalayee means many things to me but the one that is most important and comes to mind first is friends.

I am forever grateful to the founders for their vision and hard work to create this Place of Friends.

WALTER CHUCK WAS *a camper and CIT 1977-1984 and Family Camp member. He has been a volunteer work crew and donor. His son and daughter were campers, CITs, Staff, work crew volunteers and has 2 nieces and a nephew that have and still attend Camp. He works for 3 small water districts and has been a local elected official for 12 years.*

25

I GET BY WITH A LITTLE HELP FROM MY FRIENDS, 1977

NED HARDWOOD

For my first session at Unalayee, I joined the Wild Tribe for a hike to Grizzly Lake. My counselors were James Camp, Caroline Reeves, and Molly (...shout out to Molly whose last name I'm not sure I ever knew). I came to Camp with my school friend, Scott Cosgrove. Scott was particularly interested in trying rock climbing, which was a special feature of the Wild Tribe. In my private thoughts I remember feeling apprehensive about rock climbing; like, it was a test that I had not studied for. I was a thirteen-year-old mild-mannered kid. My comfort zone was hiking; otherwise, I was generally risk averse.

On the way home from Grizzly Lake, we camped at Somerville where a camp truck dropped off rock climbing gear. We hiked the new gear to Doe Lake for a rock climbing lay over. When we arrived at Doe, we set up camp and explored. James admired a large conifer near our sleep spot. He drew my attention to how inviting the lower branches were for climbing. I took the bait and slowly began to lift myself up into this beautiful tree.

James stood nearby saying encouraging things; he suggested I had hidden talents as a spider man. I climbed as high as I felt comfortable and then started back down. As I neared the ground, I slipped on a bough and fell from the tree scraping my knee and elbow. When I hit the ground I remember rolling a few feet down the side of a hill. I collected myself and took stock of my minor scrapes. James smiled at me approvingly. I was thrilled to have climbed the tree and I was delighted to have my abrasions, evidence of having done something wild.

The next morning James set up a top belay on a nearby outcrop. Scott showed us all how he was born to climb rocks; and, feeling less nervous about climbing after my fall from the tree, I had a great time too.

The comfort I feel from this story comes from feeling seen. James helped me learn to have fun and feel comfortable outdoors.

I was a camper from 1977-1981, and a counselor in 1982 and in the early 90s. I was a Family Camper when Ursula and Amanda were little, and I am currently a board member. I enjoy volunteering during the summer, usually during Opening. I live in Arcata, CA with my wife, Heather Scharlack. We met at Camp in 1984. I work as a building contractor specializing in heat pump installations for residences.

26

THE BIRTH OF GONZO, 1978
HEATHER STEELE

The summer of 1978 turned out to be my last as a camper at Unalayee. I was 16, and having gone on Hiking Tribe the two previous summers, I wanted to take it easy and just stay in the basin. The craft shack and sweat lodge were calling. Little did I know that the base camp experience would serve up the greatest physical and mental challenge of my lifetime to that point.

It happened when "Jake" counselor Garth Harwood, just two years my senior, decided it would be a good idea to offer the "Mother of all choice hikes." Understand that at that point in Unalayee's history, the longest choice hikes typically went to places like Long/Trail Gulch or South Fork Lakes, maxing out at maybe 8-10 miles per day. I don't think even Statue was considered close enough back then. So you can imagine how shocking it was when Garth and his Co David Ferrell announced a choice hike to Grizzly Lake, an approximate round trip distance of 80 miles.

I wasn't a particularly strong hiker. My stubby legs (yeah, blame it on the legs!), had a hard time matching the stride of bigger people, and I basically regarded backpacking with a mix of resignation and dread of the inevitable pain and suffering. Uphill stretches were particularly miserable, guaranteed to put me in the ignominious last position in line, shepherded by some patient and encouraging "caboose" counselor who would invariably tell me how great I was doing as I inwardly cursed my pathetic circumstances. (At one of my most humiliating Baby Camper lows, counselor Tom Marquette strapped my pack onto his own to get me up the hill out of the Tangle Blue drainage.) In other words, MY going on an 80-mile hike in 4 days was completely ludicrous.

Naturally, I signed up. Two years previous, I'd been to Grizzly on Hiking Tribe and it had imprinted on my mind as the most sublime, magical place I'd ever been. The thought of revisiting that Holy Grail of destinations was irresistible. Even better, my good friends and fellow campers Maura and April joined as well.

At the hike prep meeting we learned that every possible ounce, nay quarter ounce, of weight must be shaved from our backpacks. We were allowed one change of socks, but extra underwear was out of the question. A toothbrush was allowed but no toothpaste, and – back in the day when every kid came to Camp with a multi-piece aluminum mess kit complete with the handy wing-nutted bracket to hold everything together – a cup and spoon must suffice to eat.

Such an epic and ground-breaking hike must have an epic name, and someone (Garth?) suggested the name "Gonzo."

We started with a minor "cheat," leaving the night before all the other hikes in order to knock off the 5 or so miles between Camp and the Engle Mine. Just to emphasize how *tough* we had it back then (get out your hanky!): the PCT didn't exist. Getting to the mine entailed going up the backside of Little Marshy, cross-country to catch an old trail that contoured above Eagle Creek, following that a couple miles to the "4-Sign Meadow," slogging up the meadow to another old trail that later became a section of the PCT, and following that to the mine and the Eagle-Granite Divide. Once at the Divide, there was no engineered, gently-sloping highway to the Marbles. It was peg-legged side-hill cross-country through the forest, climbing over logs and branches, and - in my case - profoundly hoping our counselors had some vague notion of where they were going.

From the Divide, we were mostly off-trail: past Fox Creek Basin and South Fork, Buck and Long and Trail Gulch lakes, to the top of Rush Creek, where we had a blissful (to my young knees) 7-mile downhill trail cruise along the creek to Summerville, elevation 2,800 ft. From there, it was almost unrelenting uphill to the China Gulch trailhead, over the ridge into Grizzly Creek drainage, and on up to the lake at 7,100 feet.

The days were a bit of a blur, but I distinctly remember our being awakened in the dark at 5 am sharp. Garth sang "Rise and Shine" in his intentionally most loud and obnoxious voice and threatened to dump us out of our sleeping bags if we didn't immediately emerge. He ordered us to consume every crumb of our granola-and-dry milk breakfast because we would need the calories to get to our day's destination.

On the second full day, after scampering down Rush Creek, we found to our dismay that the three-or-so-mile stretch from Summerville up to the China Gulch trailhead had been recently clear-cut. What we encountered was a hot, dry wasteland, scarred with trenches and hummocks by logging equipment. On this churned-up terrain, no track or road to the trailhead could be discerned. Never mind, our intrepid leaders took off up the beach-sand-consistency slope. Miraculously, to my doom-and-gloom mindset, they found the trailhead way up above.

I don't remember the last pitch to Grizzly Lake or what must have been a very happy arrival, but we made it. The next clear memory was the bliss of sleeping in to 7 am and waking up on a clean granite slab to bright sunshine and a *hot* breakfast of cream-of-wheat in PARADISE. What joy! Then, no dilly-dallying: it was back down Grizzly Creek, over the ridge, waaay down to Summerville and up the 7-mile incline along Rush Creek.

I had been seriously dreading that climb, to my mind the living embodiment of Hell. Surprisingly, I marched up it cheerfully. It could have been the horses-to-the-barn phenomenon, or the fact that Counselor David and I discovered a mutual interest in round singing and found a wealth of diversion in swapping songs. Added to that, we'd decided we needed to compose a commemorative Gonzo anthem. I took the task to heart and used the abundant trail hours to come up with the following, to the tune of *Freight Train*:

> Gonzo, Gonzo, walking so far
>> Gonzo, Gonzo walking so fast
>> Please don't tell what trail I'm on so they won't know where I've gone.
>> I've been through a lot of pain
>> But Gonzo Blood runs hot in my veins
>> It melts the snow and warms the rain and keeps me running all day long.
>> The trail it can get pretty rough
>> But Gonzo Blood is pretty tough
>> If 20 miles is not enough, you can be a Gonzo too!

Not quite the lyric mastery of 16-y-o Taylor Swift, but it got me back to Camp.

In the end, we accomplished what had seemed impossible. As April remembers, we felt like heroes (the *Chariots of Fire* theme song comes to mind). We estimated our longest hiking day at a nearly unimaginable 23 miles.

Oh, did I forget to mention that Maura blew out her wonky knee on the first day, and *kept going*? She did, with a scavenged tree branch as a walking staff. Many years and several knee surgeries later, she has repeatedly questioned the intelligence of that decision. April, in her brand new first-ever pair of hiking boots, learned that it's possible to grow a new blister *inside* an existing one.

But we were on an epic mission. And the determination that got us to Grizzly and back proved to our young selves that one's inner reserves can overcome what our past might predict.

I'm deeply grateful to Unalayee for that lesson!

HEATHER STEELE IS A LOT OWNER, *Central brat (1969-71), camper (1972-78), staff (1980-86), board member (early '80's), and volunteer (as long as I'm able).*

27

LIFE AS A CENTRAL BRAT, 1980'S-1990'S
BECCA FITCH EASTMAN

It didn't get much better than life as a Central brat at Camp Unalayee in the late 80's/early 90's. Between making the best friends of my life (even now), befriending the coolest counselors (whom I idolized, and still do), spending hours exploring Mosquito Creek (catching frogs, making rock paint, and doing all the things you'd think a little kid would do left to their own devices along a creek), raiding any and all buildings and cabinets for sugar (Bubbie, can we please have some Zing?), and getting to spend full days and nights under the open skies with my sister, parents, and wider Camp family - I couldn't have asked for anything more. And though I couldn't have asked for anything more, Special Days as a Central brat *were* even more.

They were like Christmas, Halloween, and Thanksgiving all rolled into one! And while it's hard to fully separate one Special Day from the next in my memories, there are a few key pieces that live on for me. Firstly, breakfast. Sugary cereal?! A true treat for me, and Frosted Flakes were my ultimate favorite. Then there were the morning meeting skits. One of my favorites was when I got to be Wendy, and my sister was Peter Pan. Counselors zoomed all over the campfire pit while I held on tight to my sister's hand, grinning from ear to ear.

Once the excitement of morning meeting was over, I always knew just where I would be off to - the scavenger hunt! Time to "make friends, win prizes, and blow chunks." My Special Day mornings were spent searching all over Camp and witnessing the madness of the craft shack, and my afternoons were spent at one of my ultimate favorite places - the waterfront.

I don't actually have too many memories of dinner and the Virginia Reel on

Special Days as a child, but I do remember the nights. Sleepy campfires at the end of a Special Day, drifting off to sleep in my parents' arms as folks performed skits and sang songs around the campfire.

Like I said, it didn't get much better than life as a Central brat at Camp Unalayee in the late 80's/early 90's

I'VE BEEN GOING to Camp since I was just 6-weeks old. I was a Central brat from 1989-1998, a camper from 1999-2006, a counselor from 2007-2018 (though I did miss a summer in there somewhere), and I've been a work crew volunteer on and off since 2019. I currently live in Ashland, OR and work for Fieldguides Outdoor Education (founded by the amazing James & Jessie Camp). Camp will always be home for me and I hope my little one Wilder will be able to say the same someday.

28

STATUE WITH A LAYOVER, THE OG WAY, 1980'S

FRED LIFTON

Back in the mid-eighties, don't recall the exact year, I was working the food shack for the summer. As a "reward," I was allowed to go out on a Gonzo choice hike Third Session. My co's and I decided we would try and get to Statue Lake fast enough to actually take a layover day, before hiking back. In those days, the PCT was not finished, so to get to Statue from Camp you had to go to Long Gulch Lake via North Fork of Coffee Creek, then down to the Cecilville-Callahan road, and then up the Deacon Lee jeep trail to the Russians.

Leading any hike at Camp is hard work. Just looking after kids in the wilderness takes a lot of energy, attention and effort, and going out on the trail just magnifies everything. Dealing with safety, motivation, route-finding, equipment, nutrition and teen-age angst makes for a big mental task load. Add in the sheer athletic challenge of a Gonzo hike, and you're looking at some pretty long, hard days.

I don't remember our itinerary exactly, but I know that on the second day, we did over 25 miles, including the long grind up the Deacon Lee to Russian Lake. It was one of the single hardest days on the trail I've ever experienced. We had the usual issues with blisters, heat, and frayed emotions. I kept my game face on all day, though my legs were gradually turning to Jello, and tried to keep the group motivated and happy. We finally got to Statue around sunset. The kids, of course, found new reserves of energy when we got to the lake and were running around excitedly, checking out the spectacular little jewel that is Statue Lake.

I, on the other hand, was completely, utterly spent. I felt wrung out like an old dishcloth. There was nothing left in my legs, nothing left inside. I walked away from the happy, chattering group, sat down on a boulder and started quietly crying. I wasn't sad, or upset, or angry or anything like that. I was just spent. Drained dry.

More than anything, these were tears of relief and joy. We had done it. My co's and I had safely gotten all these kids through many miles of rugged wilderness, we had surmounted physical and mental challenges together and now I could relax. It was a strange feeling to be both happy and crying at the same time. I was exhausted and energized, both at once.

After a little while, I regained my composure. I went to the lake and rinsed away the tears, dust and sweat with cold, crisp mountain lake water. I was tired still, but now I just felt proud and strong. And very hungry... Time for dinner.

The layover the next day was the best ever.

29

UNALAYEE CAMPFIRES, 1980'S-2000'S
JESSIE CAMP

Looking back over the decades of memorable moments at The Place of Friends, I realize that for me, the campfires bring back some of the best memories. Many epic performances by our talented community put a big smile on my face. So here is Jessie Camp's (with a little help from my friends) list of *some* favorite performances over the decades. There are <u>many more</u> that I haven't been able to include! I hope these will spark your memories of more that *you* treasure as well.

Roughly organized by decade, are classic songs, skits, stories, and other Acts of Genius that came from Unalayee's Routine Campfires, Special Days, Last Night Campfires, Inappropriate Campfires, and Family Camp. I haven't given you much more here than the names of the actors, or my names for the acts, or a slight annotation to jog your memory, but I think that (if you went to campfires) you'll find something here to make you smile. Let us not forget:

SPECIAL STORIES told by:

- James Camp - <u>The Ringer</u> (I can just see those feathers floating on the puddle in the moonlight..)
- Tommy Marquette- <u>Lantern Man</u> (Lake Camp will never be the same)
- James Camp- <u>The Bear Story</u> (marking his territory by peeing all around his spot; Smuckers strawberry jam)
- James Camp- "The Other Bear Story" ("...feel my hair puffing up on the back of my neck"... James reminding us of that rich blue color the sky gets when you look between the trees)

- Rudy Breuning - "Skeletons and Whiskey on a Stormy Night" (stains on the wood floor in the morning !)
- Jessie Camp - "Honda Honda"
- Mike Wald - "Pulling My Leg" bear story (it just kept pulling and pulling...like I'm pulling yours!)
- Yve Susskind and Jessie Camp - <u>Spider and Mole Woman</u> (rolling around, and rolling around,....like that!)
- Sergio- Claire Engle Mine Story
- Nicco Tyson - <u>Pacific Rim</u>
- Travis Winter -"Zing Mines"

SKITS and SONGS

Remember the comedy team of Ben Harwood, Ned Harwood, and Fred Lifton ? They were the first crew, in the early 80's, that introduced us to the concept of random acts of satirical (or not) comedy in myriad off the wall skits. More comic teams were to follow...think Jesse Lyon and Raven and Sergio; Daniel and Kristen (90's); Galen, Albin, Taylor; (2000's); Bird, David Feldman, Cody O'Donnell, Monroe, Ben Kahn...(2010's +)

The 80's Era:

SKITS:

- One Fat Hand (Chris Williams)
- The Biffy Monster - C.I.T. Classic (sooo much TP and Peanut Butter)
- J J Koolay (Casey Ohta LEAPING up and onto the stage)
- Little Rabbit FruFru (Jim Wheeler, then later the Dennis Werdmuller version)
- Fire Marshall Bill (Pete Collins - wins the prize for Most Outrageous in the regular Campfire category)

SONGS:

- Biffy Buddies ("Every Biffer needs a buddy that's why I invited you...")
- "Proud Mary" led by Lisa Roscoe
- "Irene Goodnight" ("sometimes she wears pajamas..")
- "Circle Game" and "Deportees" sung by Corinne Fitch

Mark Lovelace's Best:

- Marcello Love Intro (with Ben Salzburg on guitar)
- Born at Unalayee
- NO COWS IN THE WILDERNESS !

Josh Bodine's Best:

- Sid the Squid
- Eat Some Cheese

- O'Reilly O'Leary -Bears version- (Heather Schar and Jessie Camp created this "chase round" the summer after the Plane Wreck)
- Burnin' Down The House (Heather as David Byrne - Last Night Campfire at the Lake Campfire)
- "Everyday is a Special Day at Unalayee" (Bill Ihne song)

The 90's Era:

SKITS:

- Jean Jean and ze Evil Cat- Sergio
- What Up Camp ? (Martha and Jessie Duvall)
- Strom Tooey (Martha and Jessie D again)
- "Coffee fe Norman" and "Sto-de-lay pumpay" (Rudy and Lovelace)
- Making Coke Skit (Serge and Raven)
- Bear Scat Skit (Josh and ?)
- TV Skit (sawing off his head and eating the brains) - Frank, Mike Wald ?
- ZAP ! (Echoing off the basin)
- Booshka with Bubbie

Inappropriate Campfires:

- The Muppets, starring Kermit (Walter), Miss Piggy (Heather Scott-Kline) Big Bird (Jessie Camp), Snuffy (James Camp) and more...
- Mike Wald (with Dorkus and Newt I think...?) mayonnaise, beware front row!

SONGS:

- Outdoor Type, Mr. Spaceman, Dead Skunk (Tommy Marquette)
- Magdalena Hagdalena (Dennis Werd)
- Bütterfly (Kermit)
- "Oh alay-oh, A-riki-tiki-tembo…" (Kristen Eshelman)
- The Beaver Song (Elana and Jasmine) I've been standing here, for 800 years..
- "Red Beans and Rice, think I'll eat them twice" (Max)
- Ghost Riders (Yippee ay AAAAAAAY, Yippee ay O-OOOOH)
- Unalayee Farewell (..But I'm sad to say I'm on my way, ai ai ai ai !)
- "Match in the Gas Tank - Boom Boom, alriiiight Wilson "
- When I Get to Redding (Bens Bacigalupi, Salzburg et al)
- Under African Skies- David Eighty on French horn with Liz Swim
- Bigfoot (Ned Harwood)

The 2000's+ Era:

SKITS:

More Inappropriate Campfires:

- Jesse Lyon and Daniel's tent shadow play
- Dick in a Box

- Ryan Koga's Weird Body Tricks
- Stanley and Galen Series (Galen Camp)
- Many *unwatchable* over the top food skits
- Flight of the Conchords (Galen, Albin, Taylor)
- Swedish Rock (Elsa Nilsson + Entourage)
- Macklemore (Galen Camp + Entourage)
- Banana-Bandana (Jesse L + Dorkus from Fieldguides ?)
- The Futurians (Bird and David Feldman) "Spoiler Alert"
- Spending Winter at Unalayee (Taylor, David Feldman)
- Family Camp Yoga skits
- Smokey Bear (Bird + Ben Kahn)
- Mr. Brown and Mr. Black (up the hill and down the hill..) Jessie Camp

SONGS:

- Shut Up and Do the Dishes (Albin and Nick)
- White Rabbit (Tommy and Jessie - Alice in Wonderland Special Day)

- Under the Boardwalk/Wade in the Water + more (Tim Mayer + Family Camp Ensembles)
- Summertime (Mona and Tommy)
- From the Basin to the Ridge (Mimi and Albin)
- Spread Out in the Meadow (Cody O'Donnell)

And in closing, a shout out to all the musical closing acts performed by campers and counselors alike: small groups singing acapella harmonies; instrumental pieces; homegrown singer songwriter solos/duets, and Pachelbel's Canon - performed by *Dancing On Strings*- is probably the most sublime music performance I've ever been treated to at a Unalayee campfire. It was the closing performance on a starry starry night at a Family Camp, the last campfire at the end of the summer. Held by each other beneath the firs and pines, warmed by the fire's glow, we were all transfixed during this moment of hearing, for the first time in the basin, a cello joining a violin and a guitar to play this beautiful piece. I can still feel the love it inspired for the place and the family of friends.

30

WHERE'S BECCA? 1980'S-90'S
CORRINE FITCH

Note: I recorded Corrine's recollection of this using a speech-to-text app; shaped it for the page.
  ~ Sarah Priestman

THIS IS a story about the time that Galen wanted Becca to come home with him. We were in Central, all waving goodbye as James and Galen drove off in the truck to head home to Ashland, and when I turned around I said to Lowell, "Where's Becca?"

We ran all over Central – into the food shack, behind the food shack, up and down the creek, yelling her name. Oh, my God, when I think about this, I get chills.

It was starting to get dark. People had run all through Lake Camp, all through Creek Camp, even up to Vespers point and Umbrella Tree. We were totally freaking out. Where was my little girl? She was about four years old. Where could she have gone?

It was during a time when the hikes were out, so there weren't a lot of people in Camp. It's not crazy to think she could have wandered off and gotten lost and was walking around and around in the woods, getting more and more lost. Or even worse – maybe she had stepped too far into the lake. She knew how to swim, but you just never know. We were totally freaking out.

In the meantime, James and Galen are driving down the camp road, and little does James know, but Becca was in the truck! She was crouching on the floor behind the driver's seat. She really wasn't even hiding, she just wanted to go home with Galen. They were friends, they were having fun, so they just wanted to hang out together. For a four-year old, it was all really innocent.

So then – I remember this so clearly – all the adults are just racing around, screaming Becca's name, and Carmen's little daughter, Ramona, who was like two years old at the time, comes up to Lowell and says, "I think she got in the truck with Galen."

I think about it now – how did a two-year old have the sense to tell us that? Thank God she did.

We looked at each other and were like, Bingo! She totally would have done that.

James later told us that there he was, just driving the truck, and he reached his arm behind him, and suddenly Becca popped her little head up from the back seat. He was like, "Becca!"

And she said something like, "Hi James! I'm going to your house."

By then he'd already turned left from the Scott Mt Summit, was already on Rt 3 going toward Callahan – so he knew he had to turn around, right away.

We didn't have phones then, so, we don't know where James is, right? So Lowell jumps in the green truck and goes flying down the road to catch him. By this times James has been gone for a while, and we've been running all over the basin, right? So Lowell drives so fast down the road that all of the stake beds flew out of the truck. We had to go back the next day and find them.

They met each other somewhere on the road, of course, and Lowell leans into the back seat to get Becca and she's like, "I'm going home with Galen," like it was the most natural thing in the world.

He scooped her up and brought her back to Central. And now I'm still feeling chills, just telling you this!

But you know, it was a really special era, those years with our kids in Central. For several decades, Central had just functioned as a place for the food shack and office tent. Everyone stayed in tribe sites. That was intentional, people wanted it like that. It had been more of a community space in the 1960s, but in the mid-70s, people like James and Lowell and John Markoff and all kinds of other people wanted the focus to be more in the tribe sites, more for the campers. That was great until we all started having our own kids!

It started naturally. It felt good. We had our kids, and James and Jessie brought their kids, then Carmen and Doug, and Gina Thompson and Fred Kronen, and more, I'm sure more, all these kids were suddenly just there. It was really a wonderful time.

They became their own little group. Now they're all grown and most of them are still really involved in camp, of course, but back then they were creating their own little world. We felt a little bit safer about letting them roam around and going down to the creek because they were always together. I mean, the big ones were always ditching the little ones, but that's to be expected, right? They also watched out for them. They didn't take care of them, per se, but they kept an eye on them.

I think the staff really enjoyed it. They were always involving them in campfire stuff.

One thing I remember clearly is that some of the kids who hadn't been to camp before and were from different cultures or whatever would come down to Central just to hold the babies and hang out with the little ones because it gave them the sense of family to have all the little kids around.

It was a great time – all except that day we almost lost Becca!

31

CHOICE HIKE WITH LYNN MEYERSON PARKER AND ED KEIFER, 1981

DONJA BLOKKER

There was something different about Lynn from the moment I met her. Petite, goofy, sharp and biting as a jump in Mosquito Lake at staff training. She made me laugh while showing me that there just might be a different way of looking at things than my own way.

We offered a choice hike to Log and Bear Lakes 2nd session. Ed Keifer went with us as the third counselor. Ed was full of the wonders of world travel and had a dream to take youth to Asia to explore different cultures. I also had two fellow students from my Spring Semester course at NOLS hiking with us. We took a lot of shit from old timers like T-Bone for wearing gaiters when we hiked. We knew how nice it was to not hike with pebbles tattooing the bottoms of our feet.

With the usual assortment of awkward but game campers, we headed to Log. Lynn insisted she knew the way, but it took us till late in the afternoon crawling over the rocky outcropping to find the way up to Log. Lynn had this wonderful ability to never get stressed when out in the woods. Or when she did, she would crack these really bad jokes where we would all groan and laugh. It also helped that we had a CIT with us, admirably capable, who found the correct route.

During our layover day, one of our campers impressed us with his fishing skills by hooking his thumb. Of course, his health form had no indication of when, if ever, he had a tetanus shot. Typical Camp efficiency of those times! We managed to extract the barbed hook but in my overly paranoid sense of duty, I thought we should evac him to get a shot up in Etna. We sent my NOLS buddies back to Camp to arrange a truck to meet us on the Tangle Blue road. I have this image of these two, almost middle-aged men hiking back to Camp as if they were on a mission from God, the sun back lighting their immaculate gaiters. That mini drama over, we settled down to enjoy the rest of our layover day.

We knew that the next night was going to be a full moon, so one of us got the bright (ha ha) idea to hike at moon rise. That way, we could enjoy Log Lake for another full day. Lynn assured us that she had hiked on a trail from the saddle between Log and Bear and could find the trail again.

At dusk, we packed up and hiked up to the saddle. The moon rising over Bear Ridge met us as we neared the top. It was as big as a house! It was a warm, magical summer night. We were all excited to get down to the Bear Lake outlet camping spot and waited while Lynn did a bit of scouting to find this famous trail of which she was certain.

She came back to the group announcing that she couldn't find it; it had disappeared! We all looked around for any sign of a trail down to no avail. With the aplomb of an army commander, Lynn said "We'll just bushwack to the Bear Creek trail. It has to be below us somewhere!" (She spoke a lot in exclamations points back then).

This is the magic of Unalayee; the night, the warmth the adventure of it all seemed to fill us with delight. Bushwacking down a cliff through forests of Alder was a new experience. This was fun and we were having it!

With Lynn's supreme confidence, my OCDness, and Ed's easy-going manner, the kids fell right into the adventure. I have a memory of sliding down the cliff through the brush, hanging on for life. The need to care for our campers' safety sustained me and any fear I may have felt at the outset lifted as the kids were laughing as they slid down the ridge.

I remember laughing and singing *The Things We Do for Love*:

Like walking in the rain and the snow
  When there's nowhere to go
  And you feel like a part of you is dying.

A part of my chronic anxious fear died that night. We couldn't see anything except the moonlight peaking through the alder from time to time. Maybe not knowing how steep and how far up from the trail we were helped. (1300 feet) But the kids were great!

On we went sliding hand over hand through the Alder. About the time it felt too long:

"Lynn, where is the g.d. trail?"

"It's there, I promise!"

"I don't believe you!"

And just at that moment, I slid down an almost vertical part of the ridge and popped out of the Alder into the moonlight with the trail to the lake under my feet.

"Oh...I think I found it."

Then one camper after another popped out of the alder above me onto the trail as if the Alder was rejecting us from its depths. We had this astonished look on our moonlit faces and then began to laugh.

I could make a lot of rather pedantic statements about lessons learned. I will leave those to the reader to contemplate. What I will acknowledge is that everyone in the group was a little stronger, a little looser, a little more joyful. We had that feeling you get when you look into the eyes of a comrade and know you have done something magical together. Unalayee!

DONJA HAS WORKED for Camp at many different jobs since 1978 in a hopeless endeavor to give back to Camp what Camp has given to her. She lives in Canada with her mountain man Doug, but manages to still stick her nose into Camp business.

THE INCOMPLETE HISTORY OF CAMP UNALAYEE T-SHIRTS, 1981
WADE LARSEN

Established in 1949 at the Quaker Center, Ben Lomond in the Santa Cruz Mountains, the founders began formalizing Camp Unalayee as an independent entity and non-profit organization. By 1954, Camp Director Bruce McNeil and others had created the name Camp Unalayee, Place of Friends, and subsequently adopted the Four Square logo derived from Bruce's experience with the American Youth Foundation and Camp Miniwanca and other organizations who used it, symbolizing the four components of Physical, Mental, Social and Spiritual growth. Additionally, lettering in the form of logs or sticks spelled out "Camp Unalayee."

Bruce had always been a woodworker and led many craft and building activities during the summer programs. These design elements were used in various combinations on t-shirts and hoodies for many years and continued after the move to the Trinity Alps in 1959. Additionally, artwork, photos and renderings depicting Camp landmarks and features such as the Umbrella Tree, Mosquito Lake, Bear Ridge and Mt. Shasta appeared on clothing and in brochures and correspondence. A biffy had been depicted as well but to my knowledge never appeared on a shirt.

When I arrived as a camper in 1962, the shirts had Camp Unalayee spelled in logs and four-square logo on a white t-shirt with contrasting color neck and sleeve bands. Ironically these are referred to in the industry as a "Ringer" shirt... They were used until at least 1966, my last year as a camper.

The late 1960"s and 1970's are the "incomplete" part of this history as I have only seen or known about a few designs from that era. Fortunately there are photographs from then and the habit of camp folks to wear their shirts for many years, threadbare or not and infrequently discarding them. Most or perhaps all of the designs had the name, Camp Unalayee, Place of Friends, and four-square on a variety of shirts, clothing and hats. Brown shirts with gold or yellow print and green hoodies and sweats with white print showed up often, although I don't know from what years. Hopefully going forward someone will recall some more of these designs and we can archive them photographically.

I returned to Unalayee as a counselor in 1980. A couple of years later, as a member of the Board of Directors, there was discussion of getting a new Camp shirt. At that time I was working professionally as a graphic designer and had already worked on some marketing materials for Camp. After some discussion and everyone looking at me, I got to work on some ideas and sketches. Sometime in the process it was suggested that Bear Ridge would be a nice image to portray.

CAMP UNALAYEE
Place of Friends

Ultimately, I came up with three designs. One was basically duplicating the traditional log spelling of Camp Unalayee, the four-square, and Place of Friends. The difference being an improved typeface selection and layout. Another was a fairly tight drawing in dark pencil of Bear Ridge, with the same text. Next was a very stylized line drawing in ink of the Bear Ridge skyline and a plain circle sun or full moon in the sky. I mocked up an exotic typeface that resembled calligraphy or brush strokes with the same text as the others. I really liked what I had done and wish I had kept that drawing. Pretty much everyone agreed that the pencil drawing version was the one.

So I then set about drawing Bear Ridge in ink. Along the way I very subtly included my initials as a monogram "WL." That's all, no other hidden or secret elements. Sometime later at Camp some campers noticed something resembling a backpacker or skier on the face of the ridge. Somehow it was assumed that it must be me. Who else? It also happened to be right next to my initials. For years I heard this brought up from time to time.

At the same time, another suggestion was about something with a boot print. Although I had dismissed it as a primary Camp image, I hadn't abandoned it altogether. At the same design review, I presented a few ideas using a lug boot print image. On a pocket, a sleeve or on the back of the shirt.

Thumbs up on the back of the shirt. It was made by inking up one of my new hiking boots and using it as a block print. I also had to scratch up the print image to simulate age and wear. Then I went a little further by imitating the yellow Vibram brand logo with hand lettering and type "trinity alps CALIFORNIA." Another touch was the heel lug being replaced with the Camp four-square. We never heard from anyone's legal team and the versions of the boot print used since then for marketing have been much smaller and not as legible.

I worked mostly with longtime Director, Lowell Fitch throughout the years as I had continued helping with printing and other marketing projects after I was no longer working there or on the Board. We would order the shirts in the late winter and at that time choose quantities of sizes and shirt colors.

Eventually Lowell asked about just printing the front image and leaving the back blank as a craft shack activity of silk-screening had taken ahold and campers were now doing custom designs for their respective "tribes" and hiking groups like Wild Tribe and Gonzo. It saved money as well, eliminating the back two-color print. Another craft shack activity was tie-dying where lighter color shirts and 100% cotton were needed. Shirts were brilliant and varied going forward and further customized by campers and staff as sleeveless, cut patterns, midriff and painted.

Lowell had also asked me about the possibility of a new shirt design, to be used alternatively with the Bear Ridge shirt. This is when I came up with the Topo map shirt. Front only and after begging and cajoling Lowell, he agreed that we could print two-color. I wanted the lakes and some other elements in

bright blue. The boot print snuck in there too, at the site of Mosquito Lake.

It is very gratifying to know that some of my designs have endured and been enjoyed by so many for so long. Since that time, many variations and new shirt designs produced by Camp directors and staff have come along. At some point the Bear Ridge design was improved by printing with bright white on dark colored shirts. The 25th and 50th anniversaries had special clothing and items made with mostly traditional Camp images and text. A number of merchandise items have been made as well, water bottles, hats and the like. The 60th Anniversary Umbrella Tree shirt by longtime counselor and craft shack Director, Carmen Diaz Lightle is extra special too. Which brings us to the 75th year of Camp Unalayee. Another milestone, another reunion and new shirt to commemorate our community and celebrate the Place of Friends.

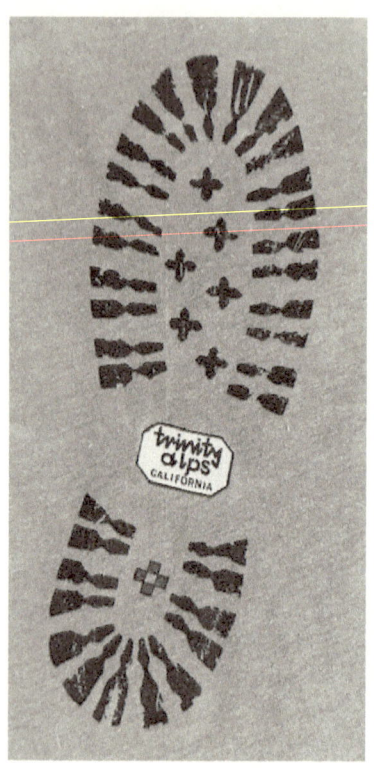

. . .

I WAS A CAMPER 1962-1966, Counselor and Waterfront Director 1980-1987, and a member of the Board of Directors 1980's and 2008-2011 moved to Yosemite in 1989 leaving behind a career in the Bay Area as an Exhibit designer and builder and transitioned to Historic Preservation for the National Park Service and Winter ski instructor and guide. After retirement, I moved to the Santa Cruz Mountains near the original Camp Unalayee site at the Quaker Center.

33

THE COOLER, 1981

SARAH PRIESTMAN

We'd gathered at Corrigan's Bar in Etna to celebrate the end of the 1981 season. Third session's campers had packed their sleeping bags at dawn, grabbed a hunk of warm coffee cake and shuffled down the road to board the buses. The staff had streamed into Bob's for eggs and home fries and then found our way to Rusty's endless peach daiquiris at Corrigan's. It was time to stack quarters on the jukebox, hustle at the pool table, and celebrate.

There was a lot to celebrate that summer, but what I remember most is the new cooler. I'd been hired in '79 to take Gina's (irreplaceable) place in the food shack, which meant I was in and out of the former ancient cooler several times a day.

Carved into the hill in Central when Camp first located to the basin decades before, the cooler was nothing more than a cave braced with railroad ties (imbued with creosote) serving as the walls and ceiling. As the food shack staff person, I struggled with its heavy door several times a day. Every time I went inside to lug-up a block of cheese, mice scurried behind tubes of salami. There were no lights. There was no drain for whatever was leaking from the storage of Special Day's chicken and now pooling around my sneakers. I'd sworn, that first summer, to figure out a way to replace this thing.

I had the chance in the fall of 1980, when I became Unalayee's director. Our budget was so tight then that we hammered out bent nails instead of buying new ones, and purchased endless clamps to tighten the parade of leaks along the PCV pipe, delaying the expense of new pipeline. Camp's office was in the Peninsula Conservation Center (PCC), which then was located in an old firehouse near

California Ave. Things were simple: two WW2-era metal desks, a few filing cabinets, a checkbook with a balance that might last till Thanksgiving, and a copy of *California's Guide to Foundations*, borrowed from the Sierra Club office next door.

I used that book like a topo map for financial stability. I believed that if foundations and companies understood Unalayee's impact on campers, we could raise enough funds to get us to the next season – and maybe for a new cooler, as well.

Like most things at Unalayee, this was a community effort. I'd never asked for donations before; John Markoff became my grant writing mentor. He'd also just joined the ranks at *InfoWorld* magazine on University Avenue, where he shared two new-fangled tools that would change the landscape of Unalayee's fundraising trajectory: mail-merge and WordStar.

I'd pedal my Trek ten speed from the PCC to the *InfoWorld* office after hours and, under his guidance, input basic campership request letters or specific "asks" – funds for new platform tents, a new truck to replace Buelah, or - hopefully - enough money to construct a new cooler.

This grant needed budget specifics. Tom Bouye and I sat on the floor of Printer's Ink bookstore, leafing through the *Whole Earth Catalog* and manuals on homesteading – big sellers back then – to determine the best design and needed materials. Tom and James were our engineers, imagining we could rip out the railroad ties, brace the cave with cinder blocks, pour concrete into the blocks (reinforced with rebar) lay copper pipe for water-cooling inside the roof structure and lay a floor, including a drain. We priced the materials – no cost for labor, as we'd just include this as a task to check-off during opening week – and the grants were submitted. By spring of 1981, we'd been granted the funds (from the Hewlett Foundation, I believe) and were researching concrete mixer rentals in Scott Valley.

We dismantled the old cooler our first morning. Yanking and hauling the railroad ties was grueling, but nothing compared to using picks and screwdrivers to remove rocks and tunneling under a huge boulder to make space for a new 4" drainpipe. This took weeks. Ask Tom for details!

Erecting the cinder block walls came next – by the time first session's campers were on Choice Hikes – so we had four days of glorified Lego-building, but with the July heat bearing down, James warned against us pouring concrete during the day.

Lynn Parker and I held Coleman lanterns after sundown, lighting the way for James and Tom to mix the concrete and smooth it across the roof.

Next step: wire-mesh shelving positioned along the walls and a dungeon-sized door attached. And a drain! There've been slight upgrades over the past three decades, but our original work of art still stands. The floor is dry, the air is chilled, and the PV-powered light installed by Ben Kahn in the 2010s is a food shack worker's best friend.

This community effort is what I toasted at Corrigan's that day. In addition to the cooler, we received grants to construct new platform tents (though only the staff tent, designed by Tom and our Swiss counselor, Raimund Erdmann, survived the snowstorms of 82'-83'), provide more camperships, initiate the "Environmental Forum," buy the little blue Toyota truck, and, thanks to Safeco, stock the nurse's shack with moleskin for years to come.

Somebody hit Corrigan's jukebox buttons for Kool and the Gang's *Celebrate*. A bunch of us encircled the pool table, ad-hoc-style, creating our own folk dance and singing at the tops of our lungs. Celebrate! Dancing with beloved staff: total Unalayee joy.

SARAH PRIESTMAN WAS on staff 1979-80, director 1981 and 82 (co-directed with Jay Watson '82). Has been a volunteer on work crew and a Family Camp member over the years. She's currently retired; spends time exploring European walks (Caminos, Fisherman's Trail).

34

VAMANOS A LA PLAYA CON CAMP UNALAYEE! 1981

ERIC GILBERT

The surf gently sweeping across the shore of a sandy cove, cacti climbing the sunbaked hills behind. Blue skies and the morning sun illuminating the rocky reef nearby where angelfish, pipefish, sea stars and even parrotfish dwelled. And a tribe of Unalyee spring-breakers soaking it all in!

This was the 1981 spring break trip to Mexico, with Chris Williams, Janet Gerrard and Jesse Gerrard at the helm. We headed south from the Bay Area in an RV with 10 kids packed in, listening to tapes of the Crusaders, the soundtrack from the reggae movie *Rockers* and UB40.

We aimed toward Baja but ended up crossing into Sonora at Nogales and finding a beach near Guaymas. We spent four days at the beach, the only people there, living on avocados, quesadillas and oranges, and snorkeling three times a day.

At night we stargazed, played cards and sheltered in the van out of the wind. We had water to drink but none for showers, so we crusted over with salt and sand and connected with the elements, enjoying nature, our newly-formed group of friends and the vibe of the coastal ecosystem.

An epic adventure!

I was a camper in 1977, 1978, 1980 – 1982 and a counselor in 1983. To the surprise of everyone including myself, I became a scientist focusing on environmental microbiology and have been a professor at Georgia State University in Atlanta for nearly 25 years. I am undoubtedly the most Camp counselor-y member of our faculty and I thank Camp U for that! My kids Abby and Coby have spent several summers at Camp – I am so glad that the adventures continue! Love and respect to all the Unalayee generations...

35

JUNK FOOD DREAMS, 1982
BRIAN FRANK

In 1982 I completed my first Hiking Tribe. At the time, Hiking Tribe was one of the greatest challenges of my life. I remember 20-mile days of dirt roads to the Big Flat Campsite, suffering in the summer heat on Sawtooth Ridge, swimming around massive boulders as we took the wrong way around Mirror Lake, and almost dying coming down Grizzly Falls. Through it all, I was obligated to endure delectable treasures such as "millet," sweaty cheese and something created by fiends in Hell called "lentil burgers."

Through it all, one dream fueled my spirits: Junk food in Redding. Despite being told to leave my money in the safe box at Camp, I decided to take my worldly sum of $22 with me on the trail. I kept the money buried deep in my pack, dreaming of the day this ordeal would be over and I'd be able to drench myself in Slurpee's, double cheeseburgers, and Hostess fruit pies.

Just two days away from base Camp, we stopped at Rush Creek Lake. That night, by accident, I left my backpack slightly open at the top. When I woke, I peered over at my bag. Much to my dismay, I could see "chippys" and deer feasting on our last bag of Granola! I leapt to my feet to scare them away, and when I peered down on the ground, I saw the tiny, upper right corner piece of a chewed, $20 bill! The deer had eaten my money!

Alas, all we were able to recover was a single, very damp and mostly chewed $1 bill. And, we all skipped breakfast that morning in light of potential chipmunk surprises in our cereal. Many tears were shed. It was a long 3 days of Camp. Fortunately for me, the bus monitor took pity on me in Redding, and I was able to fulfill my sugar fantasy, albeit in a more moderate fashion.

. . .

BRIAN FRANK WAS a camper from 1979 – 1985, a counselor from 1986-1992, a board member from 1992 – 1996, and is currently retired.

36

THE HEPHALUMP, 1982
LARRY PARKER

37

CAMP SCOTT MOUNTAIN/UNALAYEE FIRST SESSION, 1983

WALTER CHUCK

My Mom and I were waiting for the bus at Cubberly HS. I was visiting with my friends that I had been talking to and planning what we would do that session and catching up with ones that I had not seen since last summer. We heard from a couple of the counselors that were at the buses and going up to Camp that there was a lot of snow at Unalayee this year. I had signed up to be a CIT and was going up for 2 sessions.

Once all the gear was loaded it was off to Berkley. I sat next to a young camper near the front, we all waved to everyone as we drove away. He and I talked, he said he was going all 3 sessions and was a little apprehensive about being away from home. There was more talk at Spenger's about the snow and that the first part of Camp might be held down at Scott Mountain Campground. I had some good conversations with my seat mate and told him about how much fun I had at Camp and how much he would enjoy it. The buses made the usual stop in Redding and we got our last taste of junk food and soda.

The bus turned off I-5 and started to go west up towards Camp. As the bus climbed we saw that there was still snow along parts of the road up. When we got to Scott Mountain summit, we realized that we were in for a different type of Session. The staff was waving as the bus pulled in and instead of wearing shorts and T-shirts it was wool pants, down jackets and stocking hats. As we got off the bus the campers were taken over towards the campsites, the CITs were led off to the side. Lowell and Corinne got us up to speed on what the plans for us were. Until we left for our tribe hike we would be helping out with meals, activities and where ever we were needed. The tribe hikes would leave from the summit with Camp being the ending point. The hikes went in different directions than normal and places we didn't usually go to. Camp happened at the summit that year, everyone made the best of it. Strange as it may seem it felt like Camp, thanks to all the hard work of the staff to make it seem like this happened all the time.

When the tribes started trickling into Camp they were welcomed to huge snowdrifts and piles from where the bulldozer pushed the road in. None of the tribe sites were in their usual places but the snow had started to melt so there were places to set up tents. It was fun helping the kids set up their spots and we let them know that they just needed to ask for help if they needed it. The first couple of meals would be done in Central until the actual sites got completely set up and waterlines put in.

The first full day in Camp was pretty normal except for all the snow, activities were scheduled along with plenty of reminders to keep warm and to try to stay dry as possible. The most unusual activity was the swim test. Mosquito Lake was still half covered with snow and the swimming area was half its normal size and surrounded by snow. All the lifeguards were on duty and they had set up a small "swim test" area. No one was looking forward to taking the plunge but all those who wanted to did. The biggest surprise was the camper that I sat next to on the bus took his test and swam like the frigid water was 70 degrees!

The huge snow piles around Central made for some epic snowball fights, zing cone hikes happened regularly, ice cream making, glacading, ensolite sliding. As the snow around and on the lake melted, the campers who liked to fish experienced some of the best fishing that many could remember. I couldn't wait to get out on choice hikes to see what the other lakes looked like.

As the snow retreated the tribes moved into their normal sites, things began to look normal. Morning meeting and campfire at the lake, Special Day, vespers on the big log by the lake. Choice hikes went out, some destinations were ruled out due to the snow, some had snow and other themes. I went on a fishing themed hike with Lowell to the Boulder Lakes and strapped an ice cream maker on my pack and brought all the ingredients for ice cream.

A good bit of the snow had melted by the time we got back from choice hikes. The last few days of Camp were not much different than in years past. Last night vespers was pretty special with the snow in the background as the torches were lit.

Looking back this was one of my favorite sessions that I attended. The snow made it unique with different challenges and experiences. I know some of the campers didn't enjoy it as much as I did. I am also sure that my accounts might not be the same as others but one thing we can agree on is that being up there then was something we will never forget.

38

CIT TRIBE HIKE SNOW YEAR, 1983
WALTER CHUCK

When the Greyhound pulled into Scott Mountain it became obvious that this was going to be a summer that none of us were going to forget. Lowell and Corinne were our CIT counselors. I was thrilled to have them as my counselors again. Most of the CITs had been campers together for many years. Lowell and Corinne told us that the first part of Camp would be held at the summit. Our tribe hike would be leaving a day early and we would be getting some firsthand experience opening up Camp. All of us were looking forward to the challenge and learning from Lowell and Corinne. The CITs were put into the tribes to help the counselors with the campers and any other places that needed an extra hand. Staff had set up tribe sites around the campground area and a central area where meals would be cooked. It wasn't the same as Mosquito Basin, but there were activities and Camp stuff going on like all was normal. Looking back now, I am amazed at the effort it took to make these first few days work, keep the campers fed, entertained and safe.

The destination for our tribe hike would be Lower Mill Lake. We would spend a day there and hike into Camp the next day. None of us had even heard of it. The next morning we packed for our hike and put our other gear on the truck. Corinne gave us maps and told us to give them an hour head start. During that time we made a plan to get to the lake and wondered how long we would have to wait for them to get there. Lower Mill Lake sits in a little bowl east of Craggy Peak and about 4 miles from Scott Mountain campground, half the distance would be on the camp road and the other half cross country.

We headed up the camp road figuring that we would be at the lake in 2 -3 hours. After 45 minutes we stopped and decided on the place to get off the road. Once we got down and across Mill Creek snacks, maps and compasses came out and we figured out where we thought the Lake was and headed off in that direction. We were positive that we were going to get there first, as we climbed up the hill, we started to get the feeling that the lake was not where we had thought it was.

Out came the maps and more discussion, we decided that we were below the lake and needed to contour to the East and up a little more. We made our way to the new spot, still no lake. Maps out again, we had to be close. A couple of us went up a bit to take a peek into a little bowl that we saw. Success! We hiked to the lake, no counselors or so we thought. Then we heard a voice and saw them coming down towards us. They had been there for 2 hours. During lunch we talked about what the group was thinking as we were trying to find the lake. Turns out that we didn't do that bad of a job finding the place, it just took couple times to reorient ourselves.

After lunch Lowell and Corinne talked to us about their expectations and what it takes to become good staff and what goes in to making Camp what it is. I don't recall their exact words but they were something like, "Camp has always been about kids, it will be up to you to give them a place where they can learn about the wilderness, themselves and others." Another thing that helps is to make sure things like meals happen about the same time so they have something to look forward to.

You also need to make them feel safe because this might be their first time away from home and in the wilderness. We also talked about ourselves and why we wanted to be counselors. The next morning we went over basic first aid and different scenarios that we might encounter.

We hiked into Camp after lunch, it was quite the sight covered in snow and nothing of reference except for the food shack. Our gear was in one of the platform tents, but you had to climb down snow stairs to get into it. We had dinner with the crew that was already there setting up. After breakfast the next day we got the rundown on what was needed, find the water lines, get water to camp, set up the biffs, dig out some areas for tribe sites, bring the cabinets and coffins to tribe sites, start setting up the craft shack, food shack and get wood to name a few. We all worked on the list the next couple days. We did take time to do more CIT stuff with Lowell and Corinne and make sure our tribe site was well set up. Once the campers started to arrive, we helped them get their spots set up.

It was a great experience to be put in the situation we were put into that year, to be part of setting up, leaning from Lowell and Corinne, being trusted and getting an idea of what it took each year to make Camp happen.

39

CAMP UNALAYEE AND THE CALIFORNIA WILDERNESS ACT OF 1984

JAY WATSON

The year was 1983, my third and final year as Executive Director of the Camp Unalayee Association.

The California Wilderness Act was moving through the United States Congress. On behalf of Camp Unalayee and the Trinity Alps Group, I travelled to Washington, DC to do some key lobbying on the bill and to testify in a hearing before the Subcommittee on Public Lands and Reserved Water of the Committee on Energy and Natural Resources in the United States Senate.

Prior to the hearing, I had met with and discussed the bill with Andy Weissner, Counsel to the House Subcommittee on Public Lands and National Parks. My principal goals were to express the full support of the Camp Unalayee Association for the legislation, to make sure he was fully aware of the existence of Camp within the proposed wilderness, and, importantly for Camp Unalayee, to convey our fundamental need for the continued road access required for the operation of Camp Unalayee.

That meeting went very well and resulted in the following language being included by staff in Committee Report 98-582 accompanying the legislation: "The Committee is also mindful of several private land holdings on the fringe of, or within the proposed Trinity Alps Wilderness. To address this issue, the Committee has excluded private lands wherever possible or left road corridors open." Which included the road into Camp.

The California Wilderness Act (P.L. 98-425) was subsequently signed into law by President Ronald Reagan on September 28, 2984.

It was all quite an exciting experience for me. I recall talking with James

Camp for a considerable amount of time as I prepared my written statement. He was so helpful.

And, at the end of the trail, the whirlwind trip proved to be especially important for Camp Unalayee.

I WAS DIRECTOR 1981-1983. From 1984 to 2004, I worked for The Wilderness Society. In 2004, I joined the staff of the Student Conservation Association, where I am Senior Director for Partnerships.

40

ODE TO AN ERA, 1985
HEATHER SCHARLACK

During my time on staff, there was an era at Camp Unalayee that seemed exceptionally cohesive and fun. Looking back on those days—mid 80's to early 90s—I still feel the appreciation for what we managed to create together.

The staff was smaller and we worked hard. There were stressors like too much to do and too little time, rocky love triangles, crazy weather events and personality clashes, but we were absolutely unified in certain ways, particularly near sundown, at campfire.

The basin would fill with electricity after dinner, during vespers. Everybody wanted to be at campfire. You got your dishes done. You gathered your kids. You secured your light and jacket. The potential filled the air. You were not late. You made your way to the edge of a log or a rock in full anticipation of what was to come.

For an hour or more the entire camp was swept up in touching and comedic heaven. All stress or worry melted away as the body was overtaken with the giddy byproducts of deep laughter. We laughed so hard, together. The messaging of some of the old deep songs penetrated me with significant truths, like if it wasn't funny, it was spiritual. We bonded over silliness, harmony, stories, jokes, improv, classics, and respect...with total buy-in, total support.

There was some kind of mountain magic casting a happy spell upon us. I'll always remember that.

. . .

FROM 1984-PRESENT, *I've been a volunteer. I was an educator for a long time, now I'm enjoying being a student again.*

41

CAMP UNALAYEE, 1987
NANCY RECORD (RAVEN'S MOM)

My son's first year at Unalayee was when he and two friends attended for two weeks at the age of 10. Their mothers and I dropped them at the bus at Spenger's in Berkeley and then went off to my house and both cried at our boys leaving home for two weeks and laughed at the sudden, guiltless feelings of freedom.

Anticipating the pick-up day, after a time that seemed to fly by, we moms met up again with plans for pizza afterward, thinking they would be thrilled to have their favorite food again. So back to my house with the boys in time for the delivery of two big pies smothered with peperoni and all the other usual trims.

But, the boys in a chorus said, "Oh, No we don't eat that kind of food anymore," and went on to list granola, fresh fruit, hard boiled eggs, nuts, tuna, and trail mix. But, before long they bit the bullet and scarfed down giant pieces of pizza, taking extras home. SO much for the Unalayee Diet.

But, the rest of the summer did feature many long hikes in Glen Park and Camp outs in the back yard with bags of trail mix, and his two trail pals.

Raven has camped at Unalayee nearly every summer of his life, as a camper, counselor in training, a counselor and lately as paramedic and Board Member. His daughters, Simone and Anaya, began attending Family Camp as babies. Unalayee has been a way of life.

NANCY WRITES, *"I still get together with the two other mothers and that day stays alive in our conversations. We Moms love the Unalayee Food virtuous claims. I will also say that Raven's father, Robert Jourdan, and I were very grateful to have Unalayee as a fellow parent in providing Rave with opportunities to learn about the challenges and joys of life."*

42

REMEMBERING WOMEN'S WEEK, 1980'S-90'S

JESSIE CAMP

This remarkable program for women - in the late 20th Century - was an opportunity for Camp Unalayee to empower women to bring themselves and their very young children into a remote mountain wilderness with the support of other women like themselves, and importantly the support of an experienced all-female staff.

Sutie Wheeler remembers that it first happened in 1975 with her sister Wendy as director and Sutie as assistant, but the program had disappeared when I got to Camp in 1980.

In 1988, Heather Scharlack suggested to me that we get it going again. I remember this date because I was pregnant with my son, Galen, at the time (2nd trimester, so I was feeling good). Thanks to a receptive BOD and supportive Camp Director, Lowell Fitch, the program continued until 2002. I became director after Heather, was succeeded by Jasmine Monin, and then Diane Richardson and Jenni Silverstein in the final years.

Women's Week happened in many different time slots over these years: early June before Staff Training; at the end of the summer before Closing; and even during Intersession - back when there was a long one between 2nd and 3rd sessions.

Ultimately, the Family Camp program displaced Women's Week. Fathers also wanted to be able to come to summer Camp with their partners and children! (can't blame them for catching on..... "That's right, the women are smarter" *Grateful Dead*) When schools began to start so soon in August that Unalayee compressed the summer schedule and removed the long intersession, Family Camp directly competed for the Women's Week time slot.

What happened during Women's Week? Ahhh, get ready gents, the untold mystery revealed at last....

People talk about the difference between female and male "energy." I felt that difference every year during the Women's Week part of my Unalayee summer experience. From the time the men were asked to leave - and not come back into the basin over the ridges or up the Mosquito drainage past "Creek 6"- until their return 8 days later, there was a palpable change.

Female staff members now had the power to run the entire show. That included not just organizing the food, and being the tribe and hike counselors, but also doing the burns, changing the flat inner tire on Beulah half-way down the road, fixing the waterline, fixing anything that broke, lighting the hefalump, keeping watch for the bear at night, and all the work crew/Central tasks heretofore dominated by the men on staff. Yes, I remember female staff telling me how grateful they were to *at last* be able to learn, and do, some of those things ! (20th Century, remember)

And at the same time there descended on the basin a time of rest, a "breather" from the clamor of the sessions. This was mostly because there were *way less* people in the basin. But I think also, given that space in such a beautiful landscape, some kind of female, gently caring earthwise energy settled in.

We lived in Lake Camp; we sat in circles; we sang in the teepee and around the fire; we danced in the sweat meadow on summer solstice; we took sweats; we sunned and swam; we shared conversation while we watched the very young play in the Beauty; we ate fresh homegrown produce that the women would bring; we baked and made food from scratch (I remember using the *Moosewood Cookbook*'s recipes for hummus, tabouli, pound cake for the chocolate fondue with fresh fruit) ; we did crafts: made ceramic goddesses, plaster masks, paper or grass-woven dolls, beaded and leather amulets, and we had "secret pals" to make presents for at the last day ceremony. Clothing was optional anywhere and anytime in the basin. And, we backpacked- in *all* kinds of weather -and carried each other's children or the extra gear they required. In later years when enrollment grew, we created a week-long trail tribe as well as having the original base camp program.

Who came to Women's Week? We welcomed single women and couples; mothers with little babies, very young children (boys to age 8 allowed), and/or older girls; grandmothers too. Many women were new to a wilderness experience, especially new to doing it on their own with their children. Some folks were only new to the Trinity Alps. Unalayee alumnae staff with children came as clients also.

Who staffed Women's Week? Interested Unalayee staff members and women from outside the Unalayee community who were skilled in arts, healthcare, childcare, and outdoor living skills. Rock Stars, simply put. Once Women's Week was moved to either before or after camp sessions, we often experienced terrible weather during the program. Calm, Grace, Fortitude, Tolerance, and Creativity were necessary when serving inexperienced women and their very young children cooped up in the storm tents for days, or backpacking in the rain, or in later years waking up to thick smoke on the trail. Kudos to the staff those years ! A special Memorial Thank You to our long time Camp nurse, Nikki King. Nikki gently set the tone for a healthy week with her emphasis on personal responsibility and slowing down enough to be able to be present and take notice.

There are lots of stories. I remember sending baby Galen home to James in Ashland (he was hosting some of the men there for the week) because the weather was so bad and my mom, Molly Gerrard, couldn't take care of both baby Galen and little Sarah when I was so busy in the chaos of freezing wet weather as director. Sarah Priestman drove him back home to Ashland, and she later told me that it was the first time she had to figure out how to get an infant's car seat unbuckled. She knew she couldn't leave him in the van (he was still crying!) so she brought him in the car seat into a rest room at a gas station off of RT 5. Then she couldn't figure out how to get the car seat back in - but it looks like it finally got resolved, all in the spirit of Women's Week.

Luckily the men were in town and not backpacking or spelunking in the Marbles that year.

We had bears when we did the program after Camp. They would come in because it felt so quiet and empty, I guess. Heather remembers us sleeping in Central and banging on pots with spoons to try to deter the bear from breaking into the cooler. I remember hearing them at night banging the cabinets in our Lake Camps and having one run right past our sleep spot. Never heard it approaching, such a quiet stealth expert.

One day when I was in Central, 2 men on horseback came up the road. They were from the Forest Service, which had finally decided to remove the last remnants of the '84 plane wreck up in the Enchanted Forest region of the basin above Lake Camp. Thanks for the advance notice guys ! Knowing our "clothing optional" policy, I warned them that they were to stay away from the lake, and meadows surrounding it, because it was a women-only sanctuary ...or something like that!! They politely headed up the back way and we never saw them.

Small is beautiful. It always felt so good to lessen the impact on the basin for that week. What a gift to all of the women who were able to enjoy living in and taking care of paradise together. To have it to ourselves like that !

I feel so grateful and lucky to have been a part of those special weeks. Every year, when it was over and all the staff members who had been on a break trickled back into the basin, male energy would return. As wonderful as that energy is, it always felt loud and overwhelming at first. It felt supportive though, like we were off full-time duty at last. Someone else could fix the next flat tire!

43

WOMEN'S WEEK MEMORIES, 1990'S
DIANE RICHARDSON

One of the enjoyable crafts at the craft shack was mask making. Women and girls would pair up to make the masks out of surgical gauze. One person would lie down while the other carefully crafted the mask on her face. It was a sweet way to visit and get to know someone a little better. It was fun to see the different shapes and sizes that people created...a bit of personality. After it dried, the mask "wearer" would paint it to suit their vision, bringing the mask to life.

Sweat lodge day was a busy day at Women's Week. Staff members were up early to start the fire in the sweat meadow using wood that participants had helped to haul in the preceding days. We checked the tarps and the interior of the lodge to make sure all was in order, as well as filling buckets and gathering pine boughs.

In the mid-afternoon, women and girls began to gather in the meadow. We laid out our towels in the sun, swam and visited, and waited for the ceremony. Often there was a circle to bring us all together before the sweat. One year we chose to wear our masks to the circle. All kinds of beautiful characters were dancing and singing in the sun, weaving a magical female web.

Inside, we chanted and offered up our affirmations to the universe. The dark, steamy interior held us like a womb. As each group emerged from the lodge shining with sweat, the ladies dived into the lake with whoops and hollers. All of us felt rejuvenated and truly alive after the sweat. What a great tradition!

SINGING WAS ALWAYS a joyful part of Women's Week. It was a fun way to weave together young and old participants and preserved the Unalayee tradition of song. It soothed little ones, energized teens, and opened the hearts of moms. We sang on the trail and in the kitchen. We sang by the lake while weaving yarrow and other plants into crowns or while lounging in the sun. We sang in the Nurse's Shack when we were hiding out from the rain.

During one of the last Women's Weeks, we were joined by Jessie Camp's friend, Soonie, who is a choral leader. She elevated our singing by teaching us songs with beautiful parts. Madrigals and ballads rang out in the basin. She brought smiles to all of our faces.

Campfire was a lively and magical time under the (usually) starry sky. We pulled out the Unalayee songbooks to find our old favorites. There were action songs and rounds, protest songs from the sixties and earlier, and traditional camp songs. The melodies of Women's Week lifted us up and brought us closer.

ONE OF THE many special activities during Women's Week was preparing a gift for our "Secret Pal." Each person crafted something unique for that special person…something that fit their personality and spoke of the Camp experience. I still treasure the lovely pinecone doll that was gifted to me by Nikki King in the year when I was her pal.

Nikki was, in my estimation, an angel on Earth. Mother to Briana and Belia, she took care of all of us as our camp nurse. She was kind and gentle, with a bright smile and a twinkle in her eyes. Although a bit older, she was strong and sure of herself in the woods…an inspiration to us all. She took care of our scrapes and bruises, but she also looked out for those who needed emotional support or just some friendly companionship. I recall coming back from an overnight in the rain. As we slipped down the Umbrella Tree trail in the mud, we were met by Nikki who was ready with warm soup and helping hands to deal with wet clothes and equipment.

I clearly remember the day at Tangle Blue Lake when she told me that she had been bothered by a "nasty little cough." Little did I know that we would lose her to lung cancer within the year. Women's Week was not the same without her. Linda Bea had been spearheading a project to make a quilt to benefit Women's Week. Many different people embroidered squares with wildflowers from the Trinity Alps. When it was put together, we gifted it to Briana and Belia in memory of all those wonderful times in the mountains.

. . .

DIANE RICHARDSON WAS INTRODUCED to the Unalayee family while working with James and Jessie Camp and Heather Scharlack at Fieldguides. She attended Women's Week as a participant and staff member throughout the 90's. She is currently retired from teaching and still living outside of Redway in Humboldt County.

44

LIGHTNING! 1989

BEN SALZBURG

End of second session my CIT year. Late at night after last night's campfire is over and most folks have gone to bed, but us CIT's are still packing up. It's pitch black and raining but the sky periodically lights up like daylight when lightning strikes hit on the ridges and peaks around us.

Craggy is of course getting hit constantly. My friend Zach is helping me pack up my tent and the last of the stuff so we can get it down to the pile for the buses in the morning and go sleep in a tent cabin. He is holding a flashlight while I pack up my tent. We are up in Lake Three.

Then suddenly BOOM WACK the loudest noise I've ever heard, lightning struck a tree, just a stone's throw from where we were packing up my stuff. When the lightning hit, Zach jumped into my arms, scared out of his mind. When the lightning hit the tree steaming hunks of bark flew by us landing on the ground all around. We were okay (if rattled) and the tree did not start on fire.

BEN's first year at camp was 1985 at 13, and he has been coming back ever since in one way or another. Now he is an IT guy at Reed College, where he bikes, makes pottery, and plays music. He is currently on the Camp board.

45
CENTRAL BRAT MEMORIES, 1990-1996
SARAH CAMP

I've been involved with Unalayee in most ways one can be, but I have to say, the memories that feel the most important to me are those as a young child - as an infamous "Central brat." It's probably not the experience that most people think of as the essential CampU experience, but I know for me (and the other Central brats of my era) these are the Camp memories that we are going to hold onto for the longest. A small window into the most important things for me as an under 10-year-old at Unalayee:

- Drinking the juice concentrate of the '90s without adding water
- Stealing zing from the food shack
- Play Mobile in the staff tent
- Blue Hippo Day
- Playing horses and Lion King in the meadow below Central/across from Creek 6
- Our "secret" swimming pool in the creek by Creek 6
- That time Becca snuck away with Galen in the truck
- Giant stick piles in the woods behind and next to the staff tent
- "1,2,3 Lookout" at the Central Campfire Pit
- Walking out onto the ice on the lake and then getting in big trouble
- Frogs in the a-frame meadow

I'VE NEVER MISSED a summer at Camp. I'm proud to be a retired Central Brat, camper, CIT, Counselor, Program Director, Community Outreach Coordinator, Executive Director, and Mothership. Today I've narrowed my Camp roles to Board Member, Family Camp attendee, and Mom (not just to my two girls).

46

THE CAMPERS FROM JAPAN, 1990'S-2000'S

LOWELL FITCH

"There is Great Beauty Just Being on the Earth"

Note: In March, 2024, I asked Lowell to share his memories, recording them with a speech-to-text app. He wanted to make sure the story of the Japanese campers was part of the anthology, so this was his focus. The story below is in Lowell's voice, just shaped for the page.
~ Sarah Priestman

It was funny, the way we arranged it. Not like anything we'd ever done before. This was during a time period when summer camps were getting popular overseas. Like, I'd just be sitting in the office and the phone would ring and it would be someone from Thailand asking, hey, how do you start a summer Camp? It was an amazing time.

So, somebody in Japan had seen Unalayee's website and they called and said hey, we're thinking about sending a group of kids from this educational program to your camp. We'll fly them over and make sure they have all the equipment they need, we'll take care of all the logistics, and we'll pay full fare. Do you think you guys can manage it?

I was like, this sounds great; we'd love to have your kids up at Camp. We'd love that.

At the time, these were like twelve-year olds. The kids they sent toward the end were older, but that first batch was a bunch of young ones.

There were points around this time when I heard from people from all over the world. Like, people who wanted to send kids from China. They saw our address in Palo Alto, so they called, but I soon realized that they were looking for a summer camp that could set up a tour to Stanford and Berkeley or any of the other schools. Who wouldn't want that for their kids, right?

That's a great idea, isn't it? Go to an academic camp in CA and visit all the universities, see all the campuses, right? Of course, that's not us. I had to be really clear when I'd hear from all these international groups. No college visits here, sorry!

I really stressed that to the folks from Japan, and they were like, ok, we understand. We can do it. It sounds great for our kids. We want to come. We love the outdoors. We love nature.

Ok, so the first year, their plane was late, so they couldn't get on the bus. So, Seena went down to SFO with the van, picked them up, and drove them to Camp. Wow.

They didn't get there till midnight, and it was one of those crazy rainstorms. Oh my God, the road was really muddy; the rain was torrential. We had to bring the trucks down because that was the only way to get in, it was raining so hard, and we're all like, wow, this is a mess, let's set them up in the food shack.

So, here we have these young kids who've flown from Japan, driven up in the van through a huge storm and on these back roads into the vast wilderness and now they're squeezing together on the floor of the food shack. Wow.

So it turns out that, despite my talking to the organizers a LOT, something got lost in the translation, as you might say. These kids arrived in the basin with gigantic aluminum suitcases, expensive as heck, beautiful suitcases their parents had bought for this big international trip. So they all file into the food shack, and they ate, but not much, and I guess they all got some sleep and the next morning it was time to move them out to the tribe sites.

Imagine these young kids carrying these huge fancy suitcases across the creek. They'd hit rocks, they'd get gouges in them, these spanking-new suitcases their parents for their fancy trip, and now they're hauling them up to Creekside. These were like 100 pound suitcases or whatever. More than that, I think.

We had no idea at that time, but it turned out these suitcases filled with food they'd brought from Japan! They thought that we may not get any food that they would like. So they brought all this food there. Oh my gosh. Oh my God.

The organization had hired a tour guide to come with the kids. She was great, but she spoke very little English. She understood more than she could speak. It's actually the Department of Education in Japan who sets this up, and they choose the students through a competition. It's difficult to get into this program. These kids who came were kind of the cream of the crop. They were specially chosen for this adventure. This was a huge honor, and now here they were in the middle of absolutely nowhere, and we're telling them to sleep on the ground. Wow.

So in the beginning, like especially the first year, it was really hard, right? But over the years it really worked out. It was amazing. And one of the reasons is that the Japanese guides took copious notes. They filled notebooks with lists. They were writing nonstop, about everything.

So we had them for at least ten years or so, and by the time the last few groups came, they were telling us which hikes they wanted to go on. They had it all planned out. Like, they'd get into Camp and say, ok, we're going on the Gonzo to the Caribous, or sign us up for Statue Lake, because they took detailed notes about what every kid said about every hike and stuck it in the ledger, and the next year they'd show up with it and say, ok, this kid wants to go on this hike. That was fine with us, it all worked out.

And they also had a teacher with them, and there was a time when he pulled me aside and the thing he told me is really so important in terms of what Camp is all about. It's just really so important.

He told me he'd realized what Unalayee was all about. This might have been the second or third year, so he'd been there a bit. He said that in Japan, they go camping, and they love the outdoors. They respect the outdoors. They have a reverence for nature, and it's been like that for ancient times. He wanted to make sure I heard that.

But, he said, when you go camping in Japan, you camp in a place has been cleared for camping. It's flat. It's nice. Their trails were mostly paved, even when they go to Mount Fuji.

It's not difficult.

At Camp, they felt like the biffies were really sketchy. They come from a place that is very pristine and all about absolute cleanliness. So this was hard. Everybody carried their own little soaps and all the things they needed to stay clean. They were washing everything all the time.

Here's an example from one of those early summers-the woman tour guide would wash all her clothes at the faucet by the food shack, so I said to Tom, we're going to put together a little Campsite below the nurse's shack, and we'll bring a water faucet down and put a line up there so that they can wash their clothes. We're talking about underwear type of stuff, so they're pretty shy about all this. Who can blame them, right?

This way they could have a line and a whole little set-up so they didn't have to wash their underwear at the faucet in Central, right? That worked great. They loved that. So simple, right?

But what wasn't so good is that back in the early years when they were, there, well, that's around the time we had a bear problem. A big problem. We had the adults living in these big Field Guide tents, like big enough for six people, so we thought they were living large. We thought they were getting the cushy treatment, but we weren't sure they really felt that way. "Cushy" might not have been the word they would have used for those tents.

So, since they had these tents, kind of set apart from other people over there by the nurse's shack, they figured this would be the best place to keep their valuables – now I'm talking about purses, money, and most of all, airplane tickets.

So here's what happened - I am not kidding you – at one point that bear tore open the Fieldguides tent and took the tour guide's purse – and that was where they had all the airplane tickets. This was before we were doing all our travel stuff online. They needed those paper airplane tickets. Oh my God, they were really freaking out, and who can blame them?

Those tour guides are responsible for everything, and they take their responsibilities very, very seriously. If anything goes wrong, it's totally on them. And I mean, even if I bear comes out of the woods and rips through their tent, they feel like that's on them. You can just imagine this.

Now, we know that when bears have something they go hide behind a tree and then they rummage through it or eat it, right? And if they can't eat it, they move on. So we figured, ok, let's look for these things. We were combing the ground, all through the bushes, and don't you know it, we found these airplane tickets. They were in fine condition. Not ripped up at all. Just laying there, all over the bushes, maybe a few minutes' walk behind the nurse's shack. You can bet I made sure we put those things in the lockbox. Oh, my God.

These tour guides were so responsible. Like if a kid was having a hard time, or felt really sad, they really wanted to fix it. We did our best, and of course I said I could move the tribe or whatever, but most of the kids couldn't speak English very well. So the tour guides would just try to fix it – they were so responsible – and for most of the little kids the problems were really out of their hands.

This was just hard! What could the tour guides do? Nothing. They couldn't fix it. The kids just had to get used to it.

These kids had never slept outdoors. They didn't sleep on the ground without a tent. They didn't go to places far away. They didn't have toilets outdoors. They'd been hiking, yeah, but the nothing like our hikes, where you have to go off by yourself behind a tree. Oh my God, these things are just, you know, difficult for them to manage. These kids were so brave. It was so hard, and they just tried to make it work.

We had some really good discussions about this with the tour guide and teacher, like about the differences between American and Japanese kids. At one point the tour guide said, you know, American kids are kind of outspoken. They're not very polite. Being polite in Japan is like job number one, right? Their kids are very adept, very careful in social interactions. They're always trying to make sure everyone feels ok. That was a big part of what she said those kids were taught to focus on. This is not what American kids always focus on, to be sure.

And then she said that, ok, your kids might be kind of rude, but our kids aren't quite as creative or expressive. Yeah. So it was like a real exchange. Really understanding each other. It took some time, I'll tell you that.

Another thing was the food. On the trail, they'd have one rice cracker and a sardine, and then pack up. That was ok. But in Camp, and like on the bus, the amount of food blew them away.

They could not believe our portions. They were like, we cannot believe how much food you guys eat. One of the things that we do is get all these Costco muffins for the bus, right? They could not believe the size of those Costco muffins. Who can eat them?

They were just used to smaller portions. Once they got to Camp and learned they could have second and third servings, man, especially the boys, they ate as much as we'd allow. They loved the food.

I have to say at this point that we had a few staff members over the years who really helped with English. Mona McDowell - now Angelini – she was really helpful, and Tara Weaver – they'd both been in Japan and knew their stuff. And Nora Thomas, when she came up, she was also really helpful. We counted on them.

So, back to this teacher, ok, so he said it took him a while to understand what it's about. We didn't clean anything up when we set up a Campsite, right? We're sleeping on slopes that have rocks, and he said, wow, you make those rocks your pillows. You don't move them.

He said they finally got it: that there was great beauty in just being on the earth. In not changing a single thing. Earth is not supposed to be as we manicured it, with the bonsai and the sand garden, the rock gardens and all that. It's just supposed to be how it's always been, before we all started messing with it, right? That was their realization.

He said it took them a while to understand, and once they got it, they began to see what a difference it is to see how what nature is without being crafted by mankind. This was a big breakthrough for them.

He said it took them some time to figure out why we were having the kids sleep in the dirt. Why didn't we have a platform for them? Why not put him, the teacher, in a special tent? And then he said, eventually we came to understand that what you're giving us is the experience of how the Earth really is. It's true form, right?

That was a critical turning point for this group. They saw the difference between a manicured picture of Earth, and what it was really like in its untouched, natural state. This was huge. It was what you might say was mind-blowing to them.

So, then what was great was, once they realized this, they wanted to thank us all for showing them this. I said of course, terrific, yes, so how about you guys bringing something to us? Like, maybe at campfire? Or at vespers?

They really ran with this. They had everything prepared. They had a whole performance when they would teach us a folk song at Vespers. It was the one where you pulled the rope, with the fisherman bringing in the daily catch. They would act it out, and we all participated.

Then they started really getting into campfire skits. Depending on their English, they would dominate those skits. Jessie really helped out with this. They were fabulous.

And, interestingly enough, at some point emerged this little subset of popular Japanese boys. They were all incredibly handsome. It was probably the most socially dominating little group at Camp. All the girls had crushes on these boys. They became very much a focal because they could do all these different things and share what they had. Like, they could all play guitar like crazy. They all knew *Country Roads*. They'd all get up and sing John Denver, and we'd all sing along.

So, as time went on, we really smoothed out the bumps. Toward the end they were bringing like 15 or 16 kids. It wasn't like they were just an isolated little group. There were enough if them that were completely part of Camp, and they shared so many things. They taught origami at the craft shack. One of them came back on staff! That was incredible, to see him back on staff.

As the years went by, we figured it was best to have the school teacher and tour guide to live in Central with us, but the kids all lived in tribes and did everything with their groups. They knew which little group of kids were going to have trouble and how they wanted to organize the kids. So, they'd come with their notes and their detailed lists and we'd sit together and just make it all work out. It was an amazing time.

We loved this program, but it ended somewhere around 2016, and only for financial reasons on their end. The tour guides and the teacher loved the program, but that decision was out of their hands. This is one of my best memories of Camp, by far.

LOWELL FITCH ARRIVED *at Camp Unalyee in 1970. He was on staff as a counselor or work crew until 1988, when he became one of Unalayee's most beloved directors, serving through 2013. In 1970, Lowell met Corrinne Wolcott at Camp. They married and raised two daughters, Beth and Becca.*

47

ODE TO THE SACREDNESS OF A UNALAYEE CHILDHOOD, 1992

MNEESHA GELLMAN

I went to Camp Unalayee for the first time the summer after fifth grade—1992, my era of stretch pants and roller skates behind the Redwood curtain where I grew up. Camp was a defining experience of my childhood, and one that left me with the hunger to seek out wilderness whenever possible. It also taught me things like how to load a backpack for good weight distribution, how to hike safely through snow, and how to live joyfully with very little. I wait for the days each summer when I can repeat the sacred backpacking rituals and recapture the sense of wonder and aliveness that I feel nowhere else on earth the way I do in the Trinity Alps.

Flashes of images, like still photos, zip through my mind about Camp even now. Mount Shasta lit up by sunset from the vespers gathering place, first sight of a lake we hiked all day to get to, the soothing green of a meadow not yet spoiled by humans. Tastes pull me back to those times too – alpine water and GORP when hiking recall early experiences drinking straight from a spring, the gratitude of a snack pause on the trail.

And the camp soundtrack is one of raucous folk sounds around the campfire, with exuberant counselors playing guitars and so many kiddie voices belting out the words. I can still tear up if I think about "My heart is down, the bus is turning around, I'm gonna leave Unalayee on a big Greyhound," even though I lived near Arcata and never took the bus! Camp was two weeks of wholesome, healthy, formative childhood. I only went for three summers, but its impact is lasting a lifetime.

I don't remember why I stopped going and didn't continue on to be a CIT. I think it had something to do with money, and calendaring it into other family priorities. But from just a handful of years at Camp, (including Wild Tribe '94, for which I made a shirt stencil), I became a devoted backpacker. I kept backpacking every summer, and have continued to do so (with some years off while pregnant and breastfeeding two kids). When my husband blew out his ACL playing middle-aged soccer, the calculation around surgery included wanting to be able to get into the mountains with confidence. He did it, and we do.

But now I live in a city. The view out my window as I type this reflection is a tangle of electric wires consuming a sad pole, with some backyard greenery softening the ugly testament to human innovation. Instead of the floating dock at Mosquito Lake, I take morning walks around a pond encircled by commuter traffic where swimming is prohibited. Some of my friends, brilliant professionals, laugh when I ask if they are backpackers—nope, "hotel people." We break bread together anyway, but when I go rushing to what passes for mountains on the East Coast some weekends, I drag my family instead. Yes, the first hour is full of children complaining, and the drives are ugly, but by the time we find our rhythm on the hike, kids are exclaiming over bugs and leaves, nature's mysteries winning them over. And when we get home, we feel whole in a way that nothing else does for us.

My daughter went to Camp Unalayee for the first time in 2023, as a tall, poised 11-year-old. She complained, of course, because she was the oldest in her group, which was full of boys that reminded her of her little brother, and socially she didn't have the gelling with a bestie that can make anything feel great. But when we picked her up at Scott Mountain Summit, coming off a four day hike ourselves, she was dirty, feral, and happy. Much happier than any of her make-up wearing urban adventures ever make her. She regaled us with stories of the Dream Biffy, and multiple missteps of campers and the drama that ensued. She showed us the tie die she made, the friendship bracelets, and was oblivious to the mane of hair she had pulled back in a bun. Mostly, she acted free, in that way that only getting away from mirrors and consumerism can do for tweenage girls. And she told me things about the mountains, their beauty and stillness, and how she felt strong there. She knew it was good for her, even though it was hard.

She's going back this summer. And so am I. Before we pick her up, my husband and I will backpack nearby. I'll load my pack with the food on the bottom, just enough clothing, and no phone. For a few days, I'll get to disconnect my brain from the incessant inbox, the ceaseless list of tasks that keep me seated at my desk and glancing at the electric pole wires as I type. I'll get to remember how fragile life is, hung in the balance of a well-done food rope to keep bears from eating our meals. I'll reflect on how at the end of the day, we are just mammals, squatting over holes to relieve ourselves only to need to fill ourselves back up again.

The point is to find meaning in that cycle, and joy. Camp was a place where I immersed in learning how to do that. Now I hold onto its value as I vote and petition and protest and educate and garden so that we don't explode the earth and wild can stay wild.

I WAS A CAMPER FROM 1992-94. I am now an associate professor of political science at Emerson College, where I teach international human rights courses and Latin American studies. I also founded and direct the Emerson Prison Initiative, a college-in-prison program, and serve as an expert witness in asylum cases in immigration courts for people from Mexico and El Salvador.

48

HIKING TRIBE SONG, 1993
TARA AUSTEN WEAVER

In 1993, I was lucky enough to be co-counselor with David Keyek on Hiking Tribe, second session. I had done plenty of Gonzos, but this was my only trail tribe experience and our group was fantastic. It's one of my favorite Camp memories.

I've always loved trail tribe campfires—they have so much time together to come up with skits and songs (and all their inside jokes). This is the song we wrote for our campfire, the lyrics hammered out over many miles on the trail. It's sung to the tune of *Diamonds on the Soles of Her Shoe*s, by Paul Simon.

> ♪♪ It was a hot day, and the sun was beating on the backpackers by the side of the road.
>
> It was the hiking tribe that started in Long Canyon and hiked uphill for eight hours straight.

These are the days of mosquito bites and blisters,
    this is the long-distance haul.
    The way we look at a distant destination,
    and sigh at the miles yet undone.
    These are the days of mosquito bites and blisters,
    so don't stop, camper, don't stop, don't stop, don't stop.

It was a long day spent crossing a glacier, then glissading down to Grizzly Lake

We finally made it up and down the switchbacks, though our knees were beginning to ache.

These are the days of abandoned towns called Summerville,
    and heat exhaustion on the trail.
    The way the GORP has no M&Ms, and we never ever find a spring.
    The way we wake up at six in the morning, and we hike all day until we drop.
    These are the days of mosquito bites and blisters,
    So don't stop, camper, don't stop, don't stop, don't stop.

It was a long nine miles, hiking up Rush Creek, in the heat of the noon-day sun.
    We stopped for dinner at Trail Gulch Lake, but our day was only just begun.

These are the days of five-hour tours of Sapphire, and losing campers into the lake.
    The way we leave our biffy shovel at Grizzly, and scratch in the dirt for six more days.
    The way we drag ourselves up dusty hills, and sigh at the switchbacks yet to come.
    These are the days of always "almost" being there,
    So don't cry, camper, don't cry, don't cry, don't cry. ♪♫

TARA AUSTEN WEAVER *(camper and counselor: 1983-1993)*
    Tara is a writer, editor, and author of seven books. She lives (and hikes) in Seattle, WA.

49

THE FIRST AND ONLY UNALAYEE HIGH SIERRA HIKING TRIBE, YET! 1997

TOM BOUYE

In 1997, Josh Bodine, Nika Stupica, our Slovenija counselor., Eric Perman (CIT) and myself took 6 campers in the Unalayee 10 passenger van and went to the Range of Light, the Gentle Wilderness, the fabled Sierra Nevada mountains.

It was an epic hike in many ways, but it didn't start off on the best foot, hiking boot? We met the campers at my house in Berkeley and left for the east side of the Sierras. After an all-day drive, we camped at an LA dept of water campground somewhere north of Bishop. Upon arrival, I realized that I forgot a sleeping bag for one of our campers. Ouch. A ~$200 rental fee from the Bishop wilderness store.

With that crisis averted, we drove up to North Lake trailhead and took off towards Lamark Lakes and Col, a well-traveled cross-country route into the Darwin Basin. At about lunch time, we realized that I had left all the health forms under the driver's seat of the van and I had to waddle back a couple miles and pick them up. Lunch was over by then. Onward and upward, Into the gathering storm. Afternoon clouds were building so we made a Camp at Lamark lakes and set up Josh's tents. Oops, Mr. Bodine had brought 2 tent bodies but NO tent flies. One of the problems of having too much high tech gear, I guess But we had also brought Unalayee's trusty rain flies. The thunderstorm wasn't too bad and we survived, warm and dry.

The next morning, on Talus and Scree up and over the Col we scrambled down to the lovely Darwin basin and continued over to the legendary John Muir Trail (and the PCT for you newbees). Up to Evolution Basin, over Muir pass, lunch in the Muir hut, down into LeConte canyon and climbed up to the Dusty Basin. A rest day! Finally,

Except for Eric, Nika and Josh. They had to hike out to the South Lake trailhead and pick up all the food for the remainder of the hike. About a 12 mile and 5000 foot elevation change.   Ouch!   I think they got to spend the night in Bishop.

They came back the next day with our food, but Eric had bought a case of soda for the remainder of the tribe to share.   Another 12 mile and 5000 foot elevation change. An extra ~20 pounds. We carried the cans out and recycled them

Laura Ohm and Fred Lifton were our 'trail angels'.   They drove up from Bishop, got the van, drove it over to the South Lake trailhead, resupplied our 'mules' and then drove it over to Onion Valley and left it there for us when we exited the High Sierra over Kearsarge Pass.   Without Laura and Freds aid, we would not been able to complete our High Sierra adventure.

What a trip. Unalayee should do more trips like these. I understand there are many current Unalayee counselors who are learning how special the Sierras are.

Could Unalayee partner with another non-profit organization and expand our range into the "Range of Light," as John Muir so aptly named them?

There are 2 events that made this trip special for me, both on the same day. After a long climb up toward Pinchot Pass we made Camp at Marjorie Lake just north of the pass. I had been lagging the group, I had the 1st Aid Kit with the health forms. When I got to our campsite, Josh said that in another party camped at the lake, there was a UC Berkeley Professor of Engineering.

I had studied engineering at Cal in the late 60's so I walked over and asked who was the prof?   One of them said, " Hi, I'm Robert Sawyer and I taught at Cal."

I replied, "I took an Engineering class on combustion from you in 1970."

Sadly, he didn't remember me. It had been 30 years ago, and I wasn't a great student. Prof. Sawyer had taught thousands since then.   He had a spectacular career, being named the Chair of the California Air Resources board by Gov. Schwarzenegger and was instrumental in setting many of the air pollution standards for the world.   Me, not so much.

The second event was of watching a tent blow into the lake on the opposite shore.   It floated towards us for a long time.   It's owner did jump into the lake and try to swim out to it, but the water was freezing, or so I'm told. They did last for a minute or so, but we were at 10,000' and wisely swam back to shore. I think the tent floated for over 10 minutes.

Sadly, Josh Bodine passed away a couple years ago.   Nika no doubt is living the high life in Slovenija and may be a potter?

. . .

I came to visit for a week in 1970, and was hired in 1974 to fix the trucks so James Camp could spend all summer on the trail, doing summits to summits. For over 50 years, I've spent the majority of every summer at Unalayee, in fact, I believe I've spent more time than any mammal, living or dead, in the Mosquito Basin. Named Chief Janitorial Officer (CJO) several decades ago.

50

THE SUPER GONZO, 1997

BEN SALZBURG

Heather Sharlack convinced me that it was possible to do the Hiking Tribe big loop from Camp to Caribou, back through Lion, and back to camp in only 4 1/2 days. I was pretty dubious about this, but was young and strong and ready to try it out.

We had an excellent crew of mostly 15- and 16-year-old kids and one 13-year-old, who I tried my hardest to convince not to come along. I failed. We got everything packed up ready to leave a half-day early and started off going over Umbrella Ridge and basically running to the divide. We were trying to make it to Coffee Creek Road that night. I brought my backpacker guitar and played it for some of the hike while hiking by the way.

On the way down to Coffee Creek from the divide I was in the lead, jogging down the trail and singing and whistling. As I was flying down, I heard a lot of crashing off the trail and thought to myself, "That's the clumsiest deer I've ever heard!" As I came around the corner, I noticed that it was not a deer. It was in fact the biggest black bear I've ever seen. It was facing away from me having stomped off of the trail, and as I stood there, staring at it, the rest of the campers and my co caught up to me and we all were looking at the bear. The bear did not seem scared of us and turned around to face us, with a look that seemed to say, I wonder if I could eat all of them.

After a moment of wondering at the amazing bear that we saw, I whispered to the rest of the group, let's keep going down the trail. We quickly skedaddled down the trail and bivied just above Coffee Creek and made dinner.

The next morning we got to Coffee Creek Road and found that our path to

Big Flat was blocked: a road crew was dynamiting on the road and we could not get past. Heather and I had a quick conversation and decided that we would do the loop the other direction around so we would head up to Lyon Lake first then down into Union Creek then up over to Caribou. We started the long hike up to Lyon. After stopping briefly at Lyon lake we popped over the ridge to Foster and made dinner there.

After dinner, we packed up and headed down to Union Creek to sleep for the night; our first official night of Gonzo. it was a really cold night and my dad's hand me down sleeping bag did not keep me very warm. In fact there was frost on it when I woke up in the morning.

When I looked at the 13-year-old kid that morning he had deer in the headlights eyes, and I asked him how he was doing. He said "fine" in a voice that told me he was not doing fine. Heather's procedure for this Gonzo was to pack up immediately after waking up and have breakfast on the trail to minimize lollygagging so we packed up and headed up the trail. Before the climb over sugar Pine Ridge we had breakfast.

On our way down to Big Flat I noticed my knees were really starting to hurt: all that running downhill was catching up to me. I took a couple of aspirins at lunch and we continued down to cross at Big Flat and start up the climb to Caribou. As we started the climb up to Caribou, the 13-year-old suddenly said "Oh no, I've sprained my ankle."

We looked at it and it didn't seem swollen or too painful, but he insisted. At the same time, Heather (my co), said, "Oh, I have this thing going on with my knee," and showed me an enormous lump the size of a walnut growing off of her kneecap. She said, "Oh, it's just water on the knee not that big a deal," but it looked pretty serious to me.

She decided that she and the 13-year-old would evacuate the hike as per usual Gonzo tradition. The rest of us headed up to Lower Caribou Lake where we had a late dinner and dessert. I think it was chocolate pudding. The next day we hiked all the way back down over the goat route to Big Flat and then up Coffee Creek Road to the North Fork, Coffee Creek Trail, and up to Schlomburg cabin. We had dinner and slept.

The next morning we made a giant batch of oatmeal and we had to do the eat it game making everyone take a big spoonful and then get in the line behind us as we chanted, "Eat it, eat it." I think we ended up finishing the oatmeal. Soon afterward, we made it to the PCT. The kids were so happy to see it. One of them kissed the trail, which was pretty funny.

I was leading, but the kids really wanted to run. I wouldn't let them but was hiking as fast as I possibly could. They were all behind me like ducks in a row as we got past the divide and around Sparrow's Nest, Jen (one of the kids) got a terrible nosebleed. We tried to stop it for a while but really wanted to make it back to Camp so, holding a Kleenex in her nose, we hiked back with it still bleeding the whole way.

We finally made it back to Camp! Cameron, another one of the campers, decided he would look at the map and decide how far we went and how much elevation we had gained and lost. Cameron's calculation said we did 87 miles and 40,000 feet of elevation change. A Gonzo to be proud of!

After we got back my knees still hurt and I was limping around. Most of the teenagers seemed to bounce back the very next day and were fine but I was still limping. James Camp heard me whining about my pain and why I still was limping, and he leaned down and whispered "You're getting old." I was 25 and probably in the best shape I've ever been in my entire life, but that hike did a number on my knees.

51

UNALAYEE CAMPFIRES, 1999
BRENDAN MOROSO

There is no single memory of Camp Unalayee that compares to the enveloping emotion tied to the ritual of the Unalayee campfire. It is light, community, warmth and security, a feeling that speaks of our deepest primordial memories.

Years later and miles distant from my last Unalayee campfire this feeling crystallized into understanding for me when I became a parent. How to convey light and community and warmth and security to a traveler just arrived to this existence? I emailed Martha to request an old song book and acquired a guitar from a small shop nearby.

Now *Bring me a Rose* and *You Ain't Going Nowhere* are classics in my child's bedtime repertoire. I play *Irene Goodnight* and *Paradise* and call up the light and warmth. I play *Wild Mountain Time* and *Country Roads* and share a memory of community and security.

I play these songs for my child just as so many played these songs for me, and I share the campfire.

My first campfire was in 1999. I was a camper from 1999-2002, on staff 2004-2009 and went to Family Days 2017 and 2019. I'm writing from Rotterdam, The Netherlands

52

BEWARE OF BEARS WHO LOVE CHOCOLATE BARS, 2000

ISMAEL "MAYO" CRUZ

2000 was my first year going to Camp Unalayee. Our fearless director, Lowell Fitch, probably hired me as a counselor because of my educational background in Early Childhood Education. Growing up in San Jose, I was never a camper at any outdoor summer camp, and so my first year at Camp U felt like a crash course in learning how to live in the wilderness while also leading kids safely.

One thing I wasn't willing to live without for the summer was chocolate. I brought one of those extra large chocolate bars from Trader Joe's that are so big that it's like a magnified chocolate bar from Willy Wonka. Unalayee's base camp is at 6,400 ft. in elevation. Black bears are among the wild animals that live there. I thought I was so smart when staff were coaxing each other to share food brought from town and I kept my chocolate bar hidden at my personal spot overlooking Bear Ridge. I came back from our staff hike, during which by the way we glacaded on a tarp down to Washbasin Lake, to find that a bear ripped into my tent and ate my chocolate bar.

Over the next couple weeks, the bear returned to base camp at night several times looking for more snacks. Every time he caused havoc. One time he dragged another counselor's tent across base camp and took her hygiene products. It got so concerning that Lowell contacted Fish and Game to notify them, and possibly begin the process of relocating the bear. Fortunately, we all tightened up our food storage practices and the bear stopped terrorizing base camp.

So my first big lesson as a counselor at Camp U was to store food right. I missed eating my chocolate bar, but what's worse I felt bad for what the bear did in the basin. Later I found out that these sorta things happen often. The wilderness is a place where animals are competing for energy. We are co-existing with them in that environment. Since my first summer at Camp U, when I venture into the wilderness I consider the principle of competition for energy.

Taking and storing food into the wilderness is not just about making food choices but it's also about having skills to safely co-inhabit in the wilderness environment. My counseling experience at Camp U inspired me to start a small outdoor youth program in my home community through which I have led 100s of youth on wild outdoor excursions. I'm grateful that it all started with learning at Camp U and from that pesky bear.

I WAS A COUNSELOR FROM 2000-2004. Led Spring Break Trip thru Death Valley in the Chubb Wagon 2005ish, and am the founder of Growing Up Wild and Camp Cruz, 2010

53

CAMP SHIRTS, 2000
NICOLE LARIVIERE

Like many of you, I have a storage tub full of Camp shirts – long sleeves, short sleeves, sleeves cut off, some worn so thin they'd pass the windowpane test. Sometimes I think of sewing them into a quilt. (I won't, but it's a nice thought.) My favorite and most threadbare shirts are silkscreened to commemorate choice hikes, special days, and jokes with an extremely specific audience.

One shirt sports a crossed toothbrus-hand cocoa rotator - the chosen sigil of the '00 CITs, set against the ridge above Holland Lake and an expletive-laced sun.

A shirt from the summer of '03 has a hummingbird above the kanji characters for "summer" and "time" – it was one of the summers that campers came from Japan through the Ambitious program, one camper was kind enough to transcribe the words. My day off, I tagged along with a few counselors headed down the mountain to an off-the-grid homestead, and we a truly memorable number of hummingbirds. It was just such a nice day.

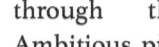

Another is from the Second Session of '06 - LarochaWalkerBout hit the trail with a ukulele, extra portions, and all the words to Avril Lavigne's *Complicated*. I remember there were these nasty unclaimed trash socks, everyone got sick of packing them from lake to lake – and so on the last night we burned them, the campers circled around the fire, just absolutely stoked to set those socks ablaze.

I like this shirt with the hands and the butterfly and the "Aieeeeeee!" even though it was for a hike that I wasn't on and don't remember. It's my brother Ben's shirt, but somehow it ended up in my shirt pile. We were both campers, and counselors, and have both accumulated our fair share of shirts.

One shirt is from my summer as a CIT Counselor – I want to say Eagle Creek Benches, I can remember standing, lined up in a clearing, back warm in the sun, laughing as our shadow "eyes" darted back and forth - "Look to the left! Look to the right! Surprise!"

Another shirt was a small-batch design made specifically to commemorate standing around Central, chewing on frosting-tinged wooden dowels that had been used to support one of Bubbie's spectacular Special Day cakes.

And of course the Fifth Square (is a nipple).

. . .

I was a kid at Women's Week/in Central, a camper in the late 1990s, a counselor in the early 2000s, and have volunteered off and on since then. Now I live just outside DC with my husband Sean, I work for RAIO HQ (Refugee, Asylum and Int'l Ops) and he works for FEMA. We have a cat named JC and a dog named Penny (got them years apart, their names just happened that way). I don't silkscreen anymore, but I still do some printmaking.

54

ONE SWEET MEMORY, 2001 OR 2002
MARTHA STRYKER

All the packs were fitted, all the sleeping pads tied on, all the campers and counselors hiked away from the basin. It was 2001 or 2002, I was staying back from hikes as the Program Director and the Central crew was very small. Lowell, Bubbie, Monika Malo & I sat at the Central picnic table reading our books in the sun on a chilly session 1 morning. As the shade encroached, we scooted our way across Central, leapfrogging our chairs to follow the sun. It was quiet, we were content, it was true leisure.

At one point, Bubbie commented out loud, "A zing cone would be delicious right now, but I am too comfortable to go make one."

"Mmmm, that does sound good" replied Lowell.

"Oh, that does sound *really* good" Monika chimed in and I of course agreed.

I don't remember who the brilliant cooperation architect was, but we hatched a plan to divide the tasks and each gather one ingredient or tool for our zing cone party.

One got a metal spoon and gathered a big bowl of snow from Creekside.

One got assorted zing from the Food Shack.

One got bowls and spoons from the Central dish rack.

One filled all of our water bottles at the spring.

We sat victoriously crunching and slurping our zing cones together as we continued to read our books and follow the sun until we were all the way to the creek. By then it was time for dinner and Troll came down from the craft shack to find the pile of sticky bowls we had left in our wake.

I think about that day often as the benchmark of relaxation. It was the comfort of reading quietly in the sun and the security of being in this beautiful place with people I really love and the satisfied joy of occasionally laughing or sighing at what a great day it had been.

As I write this in the office upstairs in the Food Shack, fighting the deadline, feeling always behind on some bits of paperwork, my brain swirling with thoughts of new projects and staff feedback and camper woes and supply orders and bookkeeping and parent phone calls and incident reports and itinerary submissions and staffing puzzles and recycling and sleeping bag washing and 7 million tasks...I long for that quiet relaxation.

This serves as a reminder to myself and all of us to slow down, read a book in the sun and have a cooperative zing cone party whenever the opportunity presents itself.

1990-1995 CAMPER; 1996 CIT; 1997-2008 Counselor; 2001-2005 Program Director; 2004-2006 Board Member; 2009-2021 Work Crew Volunteer; 2010-2011 Family Camper; 2019-Present Camper Parent; 2022 – Present Executive Director

55
CAMPU MEMORIES, 2002-2003
PHIL LEE

2nd Session, 2002

I started coming to Camp in 1998, but this was my first year as a camper when I didn't come to Camp with a friend from home, so I was forced to branch out and make new connections. This was extremely daunting for the quiet, shy, slightly awkward and mostly introverted person that I was at 16. I had been coming for a few years, but this made Camp a new experience for me. And oh boy, was this a turning point in my life.

I became friends with a couple of Camp legends (Charley and Dylan), and we subsequently took over the empty campsite next to ours. My counselors are now my very good friends (Mona and Dominic, plus Martha on my Choice Hike). I even befriended my future family members (Vanessa and Galen), though I don't have any strong memories of Sarah from that year. This was the summer I went from liking Camp to loving it. Before this, I wasn't sure I wanted to be a CIT. Now I was starting to think about how I could become a counselor so I could keep coming back.

2ND SESSION, 2003

I had a great time as a CIT this year, but my strongest memory of this summer was going on the "Minimalist Hike." I may have been a 17-year-old CIT, but I had less experience than almost everyone else on the hike. We went to Holland Lake with only daypacks, not enough food, rain gear or sleeping pads. But we were not lacking for enthusiasm. We buried 3 bean salad fixings at the divide, and made it to Holland Lake at dusk, dodging the rain while watching it pound the lakes along the PCT. We climbed Billy's Peak for sunrise and swam across the lake. When we made it back to the divide to enjoy our buried 3 bean treasure, we decided we also wanted to build a fire. In our semi-delirious state, the fire was built in the middle of the trail - it seemed like the place with the least impact. The hike was delightfully chaotic the whole time, and I loved it.

Fun fact about this summer - this is when Sarah Camp and I had our first real interactions, and had just about zero interest in each other.

I was a camper 1998-2003, staff 2004-2011, then 2013-2017 Sarah Camp's husband and 2018-present Rose's (and now Rika's) Dad. I try to spend as much time as I can with my family, and try to make it up to Camp as much as possible. Our weekends are constantly overbooked with as many activities as we can fit (camping, soccer, dance performances, ski trips, visiting friends, etc.) and it's great. Currently I work for Apple as a hardware engineer doing Failure Analysis (which is what it sounds like - trying to figure out why things are breaking).

56

TO MILL CREEK AND BACK AGAIN, WITH A KAYAK, 2004
GALEN CAMP

I don't want to take away from the backpacking skills Camp's counselors have. Over the years Camp has developed many excellent navigators and leaders, capable of technical cross-country routes and managing difficult groups. No small tasks. Yet, as talented as the staff may be, primarily, they are summer camp counselors, and Camp is more of a summer camp, than a hard-core backpacking program.

I mean this as a compliment, campers mainly come back for the people and the experiences they have, and rarely because of hiking (not never, but rarely). I admit that I have returned over the years for many reasons, but one of them is an example of camp being first and foremost a summer camp.

We were an older group and our counselors were also quite experienced (one of them even became Camp's director). It was our first hike of the session and we decided to go to Mill Creek Lake. A lovely place, but a short hike for some of us. I was 15, as were two of my closest friends, Ben and Sharkey. We were athletic, loved a challenge, and heck, what better time could there be to display some stereotypical masculinity!

Our other counselor, let's call him Brendan Moroso, catered to our 15-year-old desires perfectly. As we began our hike around Mosquito Lake, heading toward the back door, Brendan stopped by the waterfront with a groundbreaking thought, "We could take one of the kayaks to Mill Creek!"

The three of us jumped on the idea. It was brilliant. The hike was short, we were strong, and how cool would *we* be taking a kayak on a hike! In my memory we all turned to Martha simultaneously. It may have been a brilliant plan, but none of us were dumb enough to think it would fly without Martha's approval. Her response? "No way."

We laid the pleading on thick. "Please, we won't complain." "We'll wash all the smileys." "You can have the first ride…"

Martha, "Nope."

But we were incorrigible, "Please, please, please, we'll do first wash every day in the basin, and get the blue basket." "We'll even clean the biffy every day." "We'll make Brendan sleep in tribe each night."

Brendan blanches.

Martha tilts her head, interested at least. "Tell you what" she says, "you can ask Lowell."

We look at Brendan, he drops his pack and bolts back to Central.

To this day I assume Martha expected Lowell to say no. Carrying away camp property, not good for the wellbeing of the kayak, and are we even allowed to carry a full-size ocean kayak into the wilderness? I've never asked Lowell what he thought or said, and honestly Brendan might have lied to us for all I know, but he came back grinning, and like fools, we grinned along with him as we hoisted the kayak between us. This was going to be a great hike.

Adrenaline is a powerful thing, and it was racing through our bodies… for all of about a half mile. Part way up the backside of the ridge our energy began to wane. It turns out kayaks are heavy when they aren't floating. Who'd have thought? Clearly not us. Thinking things through was not our forte. Fortunately, as fleeting as adrenaline might be, stubbornness can be equally powerful and has a tendency to last longer. And stubborn we were. Fifteen-year-old boys are not known for their dedication to a task, but if failing involves being seen as weak, then stubbornness, thy name is masculinity.

So, without (outward) complaint, we carried on. We switched the kayak back and forth between the four of us, and do you know what makes backpacking more enjoyable? *Not* carrying a kayak. Through this cycle of pain and relief we slowly made our way to Mill Creek Lake.

I have to admit, having the kayak at Mill Creek Lake, pretty cool. It's a shallow lake and you can see the bottom in most places. The far side of the lake has that beautiful rockslide that goes down into it. We rarely go there on foot, but in a kayak, it was easy to paddle around the large boulders on the far side. A lake is different when you float on top of it, rather than swim from the shore.

Naturally, we created a course. Paddle to the far side, paddle back to the big rock, touch it, go out and catch a football (yes, we brought a football too), and then return to shore. I would like to tell you that in the years since I have become more humble, but this is my chance, so I'm taking it. Who set the course record? Yours truly, and don't any of you other boys forget it!

The return journey was similar to the way there. Grimacing, posturing, and relishing the moments when it was someone else's turn. In all, we got the kayak and ourselves back in one piece, and created a memorable story along the way. Would I do it again? No. But I can confidently say that the 15-year-old me would do it every time, and I appreciate him for that.

The story above doesn't mention that much of the hike to Mill Creek Lake is cross country. Or that Martha (and Brendan) needed not only to trust us a great deal, but to feel confident enough as guides to take on both the route and the medical risk of our endeavor. I know they are both skilled backpackers and I want to give them credit for that, but even more so, I want to thank them for being great counselors. They helped create a memory I will cherish forever.

GALEN WAS six months old when he first went to Camp. He has spent a portion of every summer of his life there, as a 'Central Brat', a camper, a counselor, and now as a volunteer, so clearly he is blessedly biased toward Camp in all ways. If he wasn't lucky enough in that, he also gets to work and play with his friends managing Fieldguides Inc., a nonprofit outdoor education organization founded by his parents, Jessie and James.

57

FAMILY WEEK, 2005
NANA CONNIE

The first time I made it to Camp Unalayee it was in 2005 for a Family Camp with my sister, brother-in-law, sons and niece. I had wanted to schedule a Family Camp vacation, and find a way to get to Unalayee for years. My three sons had already been to Camp Unalayee several times and my niece and nephew had also been here, too. My sister, brother-in law and me needed to make it to Unalayee and planned a lot as we hadn't really been campers, mostly city people.

I was so thankful for my sister's great sense of directions, and that we made it to the Summit of Scott Mountain, following the extra time we encountered at Weed, where we needed gasoline, restrooms, lunch and viewing the area.

Gazing at nature gave me a new awareness. We had the directions to the parking area. It was new to me to not be on a freeway or city street without cement. My minivan wobbled happily to the parking spot.

We unloaded the minivan and kept our little bags. I had recently watched the Hobbit movie and thought of how the old Wizard Gandalf the Gray was walking. I was surprised that I wobbled too.

We walked and walked and saw trees, creeks, bushes, flowers, mountains and grass. Several camp drivers drove by slowly and carefully and asked if we needed rides. The staff were so sweet, beautiful, strong and friendly. We kept saying we could make it and I pretended my IQ increased rather than my athletic ability.

I thought it was just a mile or two and I thought I could manage with my family members. Though it was a challenge with the high altitude and the longer than usual walk for me. I had erroneously added a thing to my knee — but it was my veins that needed help.

So many kids and families walked by us.

As a city gal I'd never seen so much nature. My sister kept commenting on our walk:

"We must be there!"

We made it to the camping center as it started to get dark.

I don't recall moving up and down the hill and setting up our tents or my sleeping bag, but having a great dinner that I didn't cook I remember well. And being at the Camp fire and singing, with the group and seeing the performers is in my memory. Finding my tent at night was an adventure. Finding a bathroom was an adventure, too. Many people in the darkness of night luckily pointed me back to my tent with flashlights.

In the morning I walked down the hill to get lots of espresso, cappuccino, and coffee. I brought a pound of Espresso forte from Peet's and there was so much other coffee also as well as chocolate, tea, sugar, milk and cream.

After two nights, my brother-in-law fell as he carried huge sleeping bags and tripped and fell Consequently, he had to leave early, before the family Camp ended. He obtained a ride back, and got to the Oakland music concert for relief and city fun.

My sister and I felt nature at Unalayee. Our kids were looking so grown up already. My son Patrick slept outside under the sky, stars and moon. I was surprised. Paul could hike so easily, too.

I walked slowly and breathed slowly and swam slowly in the lake. The lake was fun without waves, and seeing the hills around us was so nice, and I couldn't lose my way like I did at beaches I also tried to make a few crafts for the first time. And the food being cooked outdoors by others was so delicious. The campfire songs and theatre events were full of joy for me.

This first visit to Unalayee is so much I remember about. Rather than the veins on my legs that later were fixed by surgery.

My first Family Camp was not my last. I was able to attend again and again. I camped on the hills, next to the lake, and once near the food shack. Once I was at a wedding! It was Phillip and Sarah's wedding at Unalayee which was so wonderful because of the mountain, the lake and their love.

My latest vacation in 2023 with my tent near my granddaughters, Rose and Rika, and their parents, Phillip, and Sarah, was so joyful. A bright full moon was also nice to see all night and so new for me. Being without my computer, my phone and TV all night was also new for me. I walked around a lot to the new outhouses and finally enjoyed my lack of directions. When my tent and chair appeared, I felt surprised by my accomplishment.

Rose can hike so well and advised me:

"Watch out for these rocks and sticks, Nana Connie!"

She also performed a great event at the campfire with a cool group. Rika is also hiking so well and enjoying everything including her parents.

I noticed so many wonderful, brilliant humans everywhere, that made me full of hope for our future and minimized my bitterness.

At Unalayee I had no doubt that my family and the people I met could save the planet. Trees!!! Cheese!!

I'VE BEEN aware of Unalayee for 26 years. I'm a grandmother, still working, and enjoying visiting my granddaughters and sons in Santa Clara.

58

GONZO GIRL, 2006
BECCA FITCH EASTMAN

In the summer of 2006 at the age of sixteen, I went on my first Gonzo hike. The following year I wrote an article about the experience that was published in Camp Business magazine. It's an experience I often think back on and rereading the tale brings a smile to my face and revives amazing memories. Instead of trying to re-write the experience from memory nearly 20 years later, I thought I would share the original article that was published back in March 2007.

Shout out to everyone who was a part of this wild "Johnzo" Gonzo! And apologies in advance for any liberties I took with the retelling of the tale ;)

Counselors: John Smith, Nicco Tyson, Dylan, and Marley Ohta (evacuated)

Campers: Travis Winter, Bird Johnson, Quest, Kaydin Carlsen, Sharkey (aka Ryland Sullivan), Jordan Hawkins (evacuated), and I know I've missed a couple more (so sorry!)

It was morning meeting at Camp Unalayee, high in the Trinity Alps wilderness in northern California, and it was time to make a decision. Actually, it was time to choose a hike from all those presented by this year's counselors--one that would round out the experiences and lessons learned during that session, and one that would provide experiences and memories to last through the long winter.

My usual preference for a "choice" hike was one that led to a lake for a layover--an entire day just packed with lounging, swimming and daydreaming. But, for some reason, this year I took a different route. This year, I went Gonzo.

"Gonzo" is a slang term meaning fiercely partial, without regard for balance or objectivity. This definition is not far off. My "choice" hike was the most emotionally and physically intense experience of my life so far.

Never before had I exhausted my being so thoroughly.

But, I must say, the experience left me yearning for more.

Taking the Plunge

Their voices rang with power and enthusiasm.

"Come join Gonzo!" they yelled. "We are going to hike with 30-pound backpacks over 60 miles at an altitude of about 7,000 feet to two of the most spectacular (and remote) lakes in the world, Bingham and Statue. We have no idea if we will survive, but that's part of the fun. If you want to go on a challenging, dangerous, hazardous 'choice' hike in which we will be hiking nonstop, rubbing our feet raw and probably passing out, come join Gonzo!"

As John, Dylan and Marley sat down after introducing their hike, I had no idea it was where I would end up.

Back in the day, when my mom and dad were counselors at Camp Unalayee (where they met and fell in love), they led one of the gnarliest Gonzos ever. They traveled 100 miles in four days with four twelve- to fourteen-year-old boys and one girl. According to my mom, it was one of the craziest experiences of her life.

She said they traveled about 25 miles each day, mostly cross-country, and there were times when she practically had to drag her campers up the hills. Yet, somehow, they all made it--one of only a few Gonzos to avoid having anybody evacuated.

Maybe this was what inspired me to go Gonzo, or maybe it was that the counselors leading it were awesome.

Whatever the reason, I signed on the dotted line--the only girl out of a tribe of 13 hikers.

Starting Strong

Needless to say, when we awoke early that first day, I was terrified. Not only was I journeying into the woods with a rowdy group of testosterone-laden boys, but I also knew most of the boys were good hikers. Would I be able to keep up? Would I have to be evacuated (and humiliated)? Could I stand the stench of 12 grungy boys who were hiking 20 miles a day without showers?

The plan was for us to cover 25 miles the first day, ending up in Bingham.

We started strong, regularly rehydrating and looking forward to our first stopping point, a sparkling spring where we would rest and refill our water bottles.

I was feeling fairly good despite the smoldering heat, but my feet ached like nothing I had ever felt before, and I already had two huge blisters on each foot. I found that, as long as I kept my feet numb by hiking, I was fine. Eventually, we left the Pacific Coast Trail and our own Trinity Alps wilderness area and entered the treacherous Russian Wilderness Area, home to our first stopping point and our final destination.

We were all really low on water, but unfortunately, when we arrived, the spring was empty. Our counselors seemed unconcerned. They told us not to worry, there was another spring only a few miles away. They warned us to curb our water intake as a precaution.

It was here the day turned for the worse--dehydration and delusion making it seem like a death day.

Death Day

Each time I went around a bend, I searched for the sparkle of a spring. I stopped occasionally and listened for the sound of water but there was none. My entire tribe began to get delirious; we were all parched to the bone. But I kept going. I stayed at the front the entire stretch, thinking, "The faster I go, the sooner I will reach water."

I looked behind me and saw Sharky, staggering as we walked on. I kept going. I charged on and soon he was out of sight.

As I walked, I thought of my mom. How brave and strong she must have been to lead her "choice" hike. With each step, I looked down to see my muscles bulge, imagining they were someone else's muscles, a strong warrior like my mom. A fearless leader ready to face whatever came my way. With each step I morphed myself: my mother, my sister, Hillary Clinton, Buffy, Susan B. Anthony, Rosa Parks, my grandmother, Ani Difranco and on and on. That day I took on many shapes, many histories, many strengths, many weaknesses.

But through all my forms, I found my roots.

I found connections between all of those people and myself. I was strong, powerful, capable and revolutionary. And I kept going, one foot in front of the other, nice and steady until, finally, we reached the spring. I began to run, no longer feeling the ache in my feet or back. All I could feel was cold, refreshing, nourishing water slipping down my throat. Never before had water tasted so grand.

Gonzo Girl

We stayed at that spring for an hour, the longest break we had taken so far. We drank, ate and slept. We felt our bodies heal themselves and our minds focus. I took in the shade first and then the sun, cooling off and warming up. But we had not yet reached our destination. We still had a ways to go before we could really rest.

From that moment, I knew I could do it. I was a fierce woman warrior, and I was not going to stop.

I stayed at the front almost the entire trip. I kept pace with the fastest and passed many boys in the process.

"Damn, Becca, you are charging!"

And I knew inside, we were charging. All the influential women of my past and me, we were charging on, gaining respect, confidence and power. Showing the world we could do it. I could do it.

We had two evacuations on the trip. A fifteen-year-old boy, who went back on the first day, and one of our counselors, a twenty-year-old who talked tough, but whined like a baby about his blisters, before we evacuated him.

But I made it all the way. And when we returned home to the basin, John told my mom, "Becca was going faster than all of us!"

An exaggeration, but only slightly. When my mom heard that, she smiled proudly at me and told everyone I was leading the pack. But I knew I was only a part of the pack. Joining the influential women of our past who have paved the way for the rest of us. The accomplishment I felt after returning from that hike was indescribable.

I was now a Gonzo girl.

59

VISIT WITH A LOT OWNER, 2012
GAIL WILLIAMS

Gail Williams's family was one of the first lot owners. They've enjoyed running-into camp folks over the years.

LOWELL DAY POEM, 2013
SUBMITTED BY JESSIE CAMP, WHO IS UNCERTAIN OF ITS ORIGINAL AUTHOR

long ago we didn't know
wild haired, six packed poet philosopher
back when volleyball was king
jiving and teasing despite the score
making it fun
letting us know we were always winning

quickest...running the mountains...fishing the lakes
katherine, ethel, morris, statue, lois, salmon, devil's gulch, grizzly
    creek...

you were always game
breaking three sets of skis and most of your glasses
you and corinne intentionally losing
two decades of cits in the west boulder bushes
yes, there were those tree wells too
let's do an evac

always working with people on the ground level
digging biffies, digging foundations, digging sumps, digging snow,
    snow, snow
chopping wood, moving again ten thousand loads of luggage,
    knowing every kid

counselor, board member, director, president
working every job
working for so little

we were learning who you are

entertaining us with your
improbable but human stories
of almost dangerous misadventure
policy meeting digressions, beaten with a stick
"son of ringer," and ever exotic special day characters
none of us will forget your harmonica

outwaiting everyone and everything
troubles, schemers, late arrivals, complainers, poor enrollments,
    PCT planners
a multitude of inspectors, collectors, permitters, wilderness
    developers
and everyone's expectations

always the skeptic and devil's advocate
deflecting our attention
to human hearts and needs
to be empathetic
to like ourselves
to the heart of things

making the exception for all of us
taking time for each of us

and now we know...
loving lowell
father of us all

61

OPERATION STEALTH COW, 2014
DARA NOONAN

During my third summer as a camper, I was fortunate enough to be in a group with many campers I already knew, including two of my closest friends who I had met the summer prior. We were in our early teens and itching to push the boundaries a little bit. The good news for us was our newly minted 18-year-old male counselor seemed to be on the same page. Our other counselor was an older and much more competent female staff member; a co-pairing that is likely familiar to many. Throughout the session she had been holding things down in our site, despite being midway through her first pregnancy. By holding it down I mean the first night that she did not sleep in site we saw an opportunity for shenanigans.

I cannot recall how the idea began but once it was thrown into space it snowballed, rapidly. We planned to, in euphemistic terms, relocate a site to the raft. Think coffin, grates, milk jug – essentially anything a counselor could possibly need for breakfast the next morning. We spent vespers plotting our heist. We would move under the cover of darkness, guided only by the moonlight. If this sounds awfully dramatic it is because it was. We decided to call the plan "Operation Stealth Cow." Again, my memory fails to remind me why or how this was the name chosen but, regardless, it has quite the ring to it.

After campfire that night we regrouped at our site and gathered our materials. Materials being nothing, of course, it was a stealth operation! I remember crossing the creek in the dark and thinking that there was simply not enough moonlight to be moving 'under the cover of darkness' safely. We made our way from Creekside to Lakeside and began moving pieces of our chosen site to the Waterfront.

Looking back now the whole heist would have been my nightmare scenario as a counselor. We successfully loaded a coffin into a canoe but, in my recollection, not very quietly. Said canoe flipped on the way back from the raft, spewing life-jacketless campers into the lake in the dark and leaving them cold and wet. The canoe-flip led to considerable shrieking which, as those who have been around Camp for a while know, is a sound that carries well throughout the Basin. At some point, it was decided that a biffy seat would join the kitchen on the raft. Once the supplantation of the site was completed, we returned to our site, giddy with the adrenaline of what we had done and excitement for the reaction that was to come the next morning.

Morning meeting the next day brought little to no mention of the event. There was some chatter from Lakeside among campers whose site was missing things the next morning. The biffy seat, though no longer on the raft, remained at the waterfront. My friends and I delighted in this fact enough to take a picture with it. While I am sure the repercussions were substantial on the staff side of things, as campers we received little to no reprimanding. The secret of "Operation Stealth Cow" bonded our group and, with great dramatics, we swore to secrecy. In my own defense of writing this story, the oath has been broken many times since.

While my memory of the evening is not exceptionally clear and the feelings it elicits now are mixed, I feel it encapsulates some aspects of what is so special about Camp. Having the freedom to explore as a young teen was transformational for me. The relationships I have formed at Camp, whether or not they were formed through the planning of questionable evening heists, have stuck with me through the years. The evening embodies some of the true essence of Camp – a group of people running through the woods, enjoying each other's company, and maybe, just maybe, getting up to a little bit of trouble.

I was a camper from 2013 - 2019. My mother and I found Camp through a Camp fair at Dominican University and, among the Camps with blow-up water slides and jet skis, Camp's ethos of taking kids outside, and its substantially more affordable price tag, stood out. I have just finished my third season with Fieldguides and will be Trail Coordinating for Camp this summer. This coming Fall I am starting my Masters in Rangeland and Wildlife Management and hope that my studies will bring me up to the Scott Valley and surrounding areas in the coming years.

62

CIT DITCH DAY, 2017
AMANDA HARWOOD

A core memory I have at Unalayee is my CIT ditch day, when I was 16 in 2017. Along with countless other stories as a camper, and on into my years as a counselor (I'm 23 now), this day holds a special place in my heart due to the grit and resourceful CIT prep we had been given (thank you Galen and Becca).

Our ditch day happened the morning we woke up at the backside of Bear Lake. Myself and another camper were the elected "counselors of the day," and the night prior, Galen and Becca had pulled me aside to ask how I felt about the cross country out of Bear. I felt pretty good. We woke up to a note left by Galen and Becca asking for us to meet them at the "E" in Eagle Creek Benches on the map.

Piece of cake, we thought, and it was. We essentially were right on their tail as I led the group up the backside of Bear, down the Beard Trail, past Tangle Blue, up the Four Signs Meadow Trail, and on into the Benches drainage. It wasn't long until we were once again puzzling over the spot we were supposed to meet on the map, that one "E." I should mention that none of us had ever been to the Eagle Creek Benches. We decided to triangulate our position in relation to the E. We B-lined down from the trail and popped out in a meadow next to the creek, we could only assume it was the Benches, and we emerged right on time.

Our task was then to find the group. We started along the trail, looking for signs of a campsite. We eventually left the trail to be closer to the creek, thinking that the proximity of campsites to the creek made more sense. We wandered around for a while. We wandered around for an hour. We stopped in a marshy swamp and had our dessert cookies, exclaiming our frustration and how Galen and Becca could have been more specific, after all the "Benches" are a couple miles long, and we had no other information other than the "E" (of which there are 4!)

Finally, after roughly two hours of despair, we smelled smoke, smoke that was coming from a campfire. We followed the scent up the benches until we finally crested a small hill and saw our people. We were pissed.

We learned Galen had just left to run the PCT looking for us because they were so worried about our whereabouts. We learned Becca and Galen had to sprint through the meadow because they didn't think we'd decide to drop in the way we did, and we were right behind them. We also learned the other CIT group had been ditched at Granite, which set them up for greater success to find the benches campsite from the divide. Ultimately, we called Galen back from his search, and the ditch day was over. Cheers to a day I'll never forget, with friends like Maggie Keyek and Charlotte Corbett.

AMANDA STARTED GOING to Family Camp as a toddler. She's been a camper, counselor and work crew volunteer. She currently works with both Fieldguides and Unalayee.

RIVER COMPLEX
CA-KNF-006385 P5N7CM
INCIDENT ACTION PLAN
Operational Period
09/24/2021 to 09/25/2221
0700-1900 hrs and 1900-0700 hrs

The River Complex comprised over 20 wildfires started in July, 2021, by lightning strikes that burned to October 25th for a total of 199,343 acres reaching beyond East Bolder a single ridge separating the fire from Camp.

Mike Derrig attended the daily cooperators meetings on behalf of the Lot Owners and Camp Unalayee that summer. There was an outpouring of support for the firefighters from countless members of our community. The spirit of everyone's efforts was officially recognized on the cover (above) of the Incident Action Plan. Bubbie and Eben Bedford were honored by firefighters during "operation cookie drop" at the main fire camp in Etna. They arrived with hundreds of cookies delivered freshly baked on behalf of the friends of Camp Unalayee.

– Curtis Koppel

64

FLASH OF DEATH, 2021
NEWT COHEN

Crackle! Crackle! Boom! The noise of distant thunder rumbled but came ever nearer as I snuck out from the cover of the trees to watch for flashes of lightning. I had no idea that within an hour my heart would be beating like a drum and my ankle would be killing me.

Right next to the trees there was a wide, green, meadow with a long flat limestone slab sitting in the center.

The thunder came rolling across the mountains and wet patches began to appear as it started to pour. I looked up at the dark and stormy sky where you almost see rain falling from the clouds. I felt like the sky, excitement building inside me starting to spill out like the rain from the sky. I felt the raindrops freckling my face and arms, and the world smelt like damp earth.

After many more flashes of lightning and when the thunder was getting louder and louder, when it was clear the storm was getting closer, I went back to the cover of the trees.

The whole backpacking group was sitting under a fir tree when it happened. A blueish flash of lightning like 1,000 cameras all flashing in the dead of night. It was so bright it seemed like the world was ending. Dead silence for a second then the thunder came. It was the loudest noise I ever heard. Spine chilling and horrible, like the monster of noise was chasing us deadly close and angry.

We all jumped up and sprinted to the rock. My ankle got crushed by a falling branch, but I kept running even though my eyes were watering with pain.

"Wow," I breathed.

We all saw it. A cloud, white as freshly fallen snow, was rolling along the path at the opposite end of the flat wide boulder. It was as if the sky was at war with the ground, and the cloud was an army of the sky.

When the cloud had passed the sky was also getting lighter. The sun emerged from behind the clouds its warm rays making everything sparkle. Victory for the sky!

NEWT COHEN HAS BEEN *a camper since 2021, and spent two sessions at Camp in 2024. He is now in 9th grade.*

65

A GATHERING OF FRIENDS, 2024
LONNA LEWIS BLODGETT

There is a place in our hearts and our utmost being to seek out the companionship of others. There are times in our lives we seek the support and comfort of sharing our lives together. It is a teaching that is given from parent to child that we create bonds of friendship, understanding, trust and goodwill.

We share this bond of friendship in the founding of Camp Unalayee. It is a space close to our hearts, where the brightest promise for our future "our children" are brought together in the company of each other to "gather in friendship" – Camp Unalayee carries the literal meaning "A Gathering of Friends."

Nature expresses herself freely and without judgmental or discretionary restraint. Her actions are absolute in its resolve as she lays the threads that hold and define life. Her tapestry is a "weave" of who we are in the moment. Nature draws her impetus from the past to create in the now, so to embrace what is to come. It is a fine and noble act to embrace this wisdom, knowing that what we are and what we do is what fuels change. Change is a moment when everything is vulnerable and susceptible of how Nature's weave exists - we and what we create are one of the threads interlocked within the pattern.

Words are like the breath of who we are. We breathe in to take in the life we need, and breathe out to give back to the world what we have assimilated. Each word has a meaning to everyone and everything within its place of being in Nature's "weave." Words are threads that act like guides that are the chimes, the call, the drum, the thunder, the repose, the joy, the sadness and struggle of our collective and accumulated history. They can bring together and they can divide. The importance being that our words honor Nature's "weave" with the strength and dignity it so deserves in our efforts to find our own truth.

The truth is Unalayee is a golden word in the thread of Nature's "weave." It has brought the beautiful color of love and gratitude in helping children of this world grow in their appreciation of friendship. Its name represents the history of and imbues the intention of this meaningful expression which means so much to so many. It has been a continuous and unifying word from its chosen place that befits the intention to teach our children the meaning of friendship. If you remove the word "Unalayee" you will forever alter the golden intention that it was founded upon and dishonor those who have given their devotion in striving for its success in the past. You will lose the thread of meaning, the vitality of all the vigilance that has overseen its purpose and will eliminate how this chosen word has manifested in Nature's "weave." You will be disregarding the most honorable purpose and design it has represented from the Camp's inception. You will violate exactly what you are endeavoring to teach our children.

Unalayee is a good word with a long and valuable history and is golden in its meaning. Do not mistake the bias of those who cannot see the "gold" of its sincerity and design with the true and empowering strength it holds.

I implore you to be prudent, enlightened and mindful in your use of names as you are with your intention to our children. BE GOLDEN! and shine with what you have created. This thread in Nature's "weave" is a testament to the good in this world.

LONNA AND BOB are long-time friends of Unalayee. They generously hosted memorable board events at their private family retreat, the Monarch Cove, in Capitola. In the 60's, Lonna was a songwriter and folk musician. She performed at the Berkeley Folk Festival immediately after Richie Havens. Lonna is a published author, poet, passionate healer, and spiritual keeper of words.

66

7000 WAYS TO SAY FRIEND, PART 1, 2024
CURTIS KOPPEL

O ᎤᎾᎵᎢ is One Way to Say Friend.

ᏣᎳᎩ ᎦᏬᏂᎯᏍᏗ 'Tsalagi Gawonihisdi' is the syllabary language of the Cherokee people.

The word "Cherokee" is a variation of the word "Tsalagi," which Cherokee commonly use to identify themselves today.

ᎤᎾᎵᎢ is one word for **friend** written in the Cherokee Syllabary Language.

UNALII is the word ᎤᎾᎵᎢ when transcribed into the Latin alphabet.

U NA LI I sounds like **U NA LE E** when speaking the syllables for the word ᎤᎾᎵᎢ.

If you want to hear the word for friend pronounced in the Cherokee language you can visit Cherokee word of the week: *https://www.youtube.com/watch?v=FhLU8UVHrLo*

The Cherokee Nation is now recognized as a leader in language revitalization. The United Nations International Decade of Indigenous Languages was recently launched by UNESCO and hosted by the Cherokee Nation in Oklahoma. The initiative draws global attention to the critical situation of many Indigenous languages and to mobilize resources.

The Cherokee Nation is estimated to have 440,000 citizens with the largest Nation by population in the US. Many Cherokee citizens live in Oklahoma, while the majority live 'at large' and reside in every state. California has the largest population of Native Americans in the US, and approximately 27,000 Cherokee Citizens currently live 'at large' in California.

Principal Chief Chuck Hoskin, Jr., speaks often about the Cherokee language revitalization initiative. He explains how imperative the language initiative is to the preservation of Cherokee culture and knowledge. There are approximately 2000 native Cherokee speakers alive today and they are mostly over the age of 70. With renewed commitment to Cherokee language revitalization the future of their native language is improving.

The Yurok of California is another example of commitment to their native language. With only 20 fluent speakers and 12 semi-fluent speakers remaining, the last known Yurok native speaker died in 2013. After a decade of language restoration activities, the Yurok recently documented there are now only 11 fluent speakers, but now have 37 advanced speakers, 60 intermediate speakers and approximately 311 basic speakers.

The Yurok is California's largest <u>Native American Tribe with more than 6400 members</u>. The confluence of the Trinity River with the Klamath locates the Yurok reservation stretching approximately 45 miles downriver to its entry into the Pacific. The ancestral lands of the Yurok people are downriver on the Klamath. The site of Camp Unalayee is located at the headwaters of the Trinity and the Klamath Rivers. The name Yurok originates from a term meaning 'downriver' or 'downstream.'

How cultures preserve languages and words is complex for all 7000 ways to say 'friend.' The word *"too'mar"* is a way to say friend in the Yurok language. The word *'Unalii'* is one of multiple ways to say friend in the Cherokee language.

The word **Unalayee** meaning "place of friends" is an unambiguous term. While not found in the English Lexicon or the Cherokee Language Dictionary, a Google search for the word **Unalayee** currently returns approximately 5000 results in half a second. These results establish a significant presence for a word meaning, "Place of Friends."

Unambiguous words in a search query do not have two or more ambiguous meanings. This is important even when unfamiliar with the name Unalayee.

English is among the largest languages with more than 171,000 words. It should be no surprise that all languages contain loan or borrowed words from other cultures. The English language is no exception.

Looking at the multilingual complexity of English gives great insight into how richly flavored and inclusive the language really is.

"English has been borrowing words from other languages since its infancy. As many as 350 other languages are represented and their linguistic contributions make up about 80% of English."

Unalayee may have originated from "Unalii," a Cherokee word for friend as we have long been told. From the lessons of our elders, we have a window into our collective history. The window on linguistic diversity is closing as many Indigenous languages are at risk of extinction.

Saving 7000 ways to say "friend" preserves language diversity for words like ᎠᏓᎵᎢ. Tragically one of 7000 ways to say "friend" becomes extinct every other week. Indigenous Language Revitalization is a global initiative. As friends and advocates, we can learn more about language and Indigenous language initiatives.

AMERICAN FRIENDS SERVICE Committee *was awarded the Nobel Peace Prize in 1947.*
The Nobel Prize Motivation:
"for their pioneering work in the international peace movement and compassionate effort to relieve human suffering, thereby promoting the fraternity between nations"
Camp was founded by Friends Service Committee in 1949.
In 1954, Josephine Duveneck was present at the Pacific Yearly Meeting when Friends adopted the name Camp Unalayee, "Place of Friends."

7001 WAYS TO SAY FRIEND, PART 2, 2024
CURTIS KOPPEL

The profound diversity of human language reflects not just the multitude of societies and cultures, but also the intrinsic human need to form connections and build communities. With over 7000 languages spoken worldwide, each offers a unique lens through which we understand and experience the world. The word 'friend' embodies this universal desire for connection, taking on thousands of forms, each resonating with the cultural nuances and shared histories of the people who speak to them.

The story of Unalayee, derived from a Native American term for 'friend', is a testament to the power of language as a bridge between individuals and communities. It was embraced by Josephine Duveneck and her colleagues as they sought to promote social justice and environmental stewardship through a nonprofit organization, reflecting their commitment to friendship and collaboration.

Today, the urgency to preserve linguistic diversity is greater than ever, as highlighted by UNESCO's efforts to protect endangered Indigenous languages. The Yurok Tribe's language revitalization efforts illustrate the challenges faced in this endeavor. From the brink of losing their linguistic heritage with only a handful of fluent speakers remaining, they have made significant strides in increasing the number of speakers at various proficiency levels. This progress is crucial not only for the preservation of their language but also for maintaining their cultural identity and heritage.

Similarly, the Cherokee Nation, with a substantial population spread across the United States, highlights the spirit and adaptability of Native American communities. Despite historical adversities, they continue to thrive and revitalize their language and culture. The Cherokee and Yurok stories are but two examples of the broader narrative of the critical importance of language in sustaining the rich tapestry of human experience. As we move forward, it is imperative that we support these efforts to ensure that future generations preserve 7000 ways to say friend.

The Cherokee Nation's commitment to language revitalization is a resilient example of cultural preservation. With the support of initiatives like the United Nations International Decade of Indigenous Languages, the Cherokee are leading efforts to sustain and nurture their language, which is a vital aspect of their identity. The Cherokee language, with its native speakers is a repository of the nation's collective memory and wisdom, particularly as many speakers are elders over the age of 70. The language's vitality is crucial for maintaining the cultural fabric and knowledge of the Cherokee people.

The word "Unalayee"—meaning a place of friends—resonates with the essence of community and connection. It is a tribute to the power of language in forging bonds and preserving heritage. English, with its vast lexicon, has always been a linguistic mosaic, enriched by words from diverse cultures. This inclusivity reflects the dynamic nature of language and its ability to evolve and adapt over time.

The Yurok people's relationship with the Klamath River is a reminder of the deep ties between language, land, and life. For millennia, the Yurok have lived along the river, a place they know to be sacred. Their language and traditions, like our shared principle of 'Leave No Trace,' embody respect for nature and the interconnectedness of all life. In preserving their language and way of life, the Yurok, like the Cherokee, remind us of the intrinsic value of Indigenous cultures and the importance of their continued revitalization for future generations.

The concept of "Unalayee" as a "Place of Friends" is a poignant reminder of the connections between language, culture, and community. The Cherokee word "Unalii," meaning friend, encapsulates the spirit that is essential to human relationships and cultural preservation. The alarming rate at which Indigenous languages are disappearing is a call to action for language revitalization efforts worldwide. These languages are not merely means of communication; they are the living expressions of a people's history, philosophy, and art.

In every utterance of "Unalii," and in every effort to preserve such precious linguistic heritage, there is a reaffirmation of the belief that our shared humanity is enriched by the diversity of our voices. Unalayee stands as a dedication to the enduring power of friendship and the importance of safeguarding the treasures that connect us to our past and to each other.

The elders among Indigenous communities are the keepers of knowledge, language, and lived wisdom. They provide guidance and pass their teachings to future generations.

The past Nobel Peace Prize-winning work of the American Friends Service Committee exemplifies the impact that a group of friends, united by a common cause, can have on the world. The wisdom and experiences of those who preceded us also serve as valuable guides.

A place is not an empty landscape. Place holds people, stories, and traditions. Place connects individuals, communities, and Nations. Place has witnessed countless generations. We are place. **Unalayee** is a 'Place of Friends' wherever we gather.

Curtis Koppel writes, "My research was made possible from this original Cherokee-English dictionary, first published in 1975 by Durbin Feeling."

Page 317. <u>Non-singular kinship terms.</u> Some kinship terms, as well as a few other nouns referring to persons, do not exhibit singular forms. A noun of this type is "friend," shown in Paradigm Six. U NA LI I "they – friends"

CHEROKEE-ENGLISH DICTIONARY
https://www.cherokeedictionary.net/grammar
by Durbin Feeling, Copyright 1975, Heritage Printing Tahlequah, Oklahoma

GONE TOO SOON

The following stories and poems celebrate and honor those we've lost from our Unalayee community.

68

RUDY BREUNING
1962-2022

Rudy "Bob" Breuning was one of the first staff members I met my first year at Camp in 1991. I was drawn in by his impeccable wit and coyote spirit right away. I honestly think that the endorphin release I experienced that first summer due to laughing so much is one of the things that cemented my connection to Camp for years to come. Much of that endorphin release was due to Rudy's sense of humor. Rudy, despite that ever-ready wit, was also a very deep guy with a strong connection to nature and a great deal of sage wisdom.

He was extremely intelligent, well-read and engaged in current social and political events. Bigfoot was his guy. He also had very strong opinions and would not hesitate to share them. I remember visiting him in Humboldt in the early years of my Camp experience and having one of my more stressful composting toilet experiences as his words reverberated in my head while on the can, "Whatever you do – do NOT pee in the compost toilet." I remember thinking, "this guy clearly doesn't understand how women's bodies work!"

Well, that was many years before he became a loving husband and father to daughters, and eventually a grandfather as well. I kept in touch with him over the years, mostly thanks to Facebook, and I was very happy to see him at James Camp's memorial up at Camp in 2019. It felt like no time at all since we had hung out and shared deep belly laughs.

I frequently connected with him on Facebook, so was deeply shocked when I got the news that he had passed away. He had kept his diagnosis and his ensuing struggle very private from those outside his immediate circle. I almost had gone to visit him at Burnt Ranch and stay at his cool campground in 2021 but then decided to go home back to the Bay Area via a different route – yet another reminder to not snooze on visiting people you love.

Rudy died a warrior's death – he did not want to draw out his suffering or that of his caregivers, nor get the outside world involved in handling his exit. I have so much respect for him and how he chose to meet the Big Sasquatch in the Sky on his own terms. He will forever be remembered, with laughter alongside the tears, by the many friends and family who cherished him.

ELANA DUSSÉ (formerly Vollen) worked at Camp U from 1991-1999 as counselor, program director, CIT trainer, etc. Now living in Woodside, CA with husband Steve and beloved dog and cat, working in the field of psychedelic-assisted therapy.

69

JOSH "SID THE SQUID" BODINE
1964-2017

Josh always showed up to staff training with a plastic milk crate filled with books—sometimes two crates, enough to last him through the summer. There were the usual Edward Abbey books we were all reading, but there were more esoteric titles as well. Josh had quite an intellect, but covered it by being folksy. I suspect he didn't want to come off sounding like a jerk.

Josh's philosophy for road trips—and for life—seemed to boil down to: Make sure you have all the gear so you are prepared to have all the fun. He's the reason I have two pairs of hiking books, kayaking booties, a camp stove, tent, spice kit, folding lounge chair, and frisbee in the trunk of my car at all times. It's all stored two plastic milk crates, of course.

Josh and I never co-ed a tribe together, but we did lead a number of hikes—often Gonzos, hard hikes with long-mileage days and a group that always seemed to consist of sixteen-year-old boys. In these situations, it was not uncommon for the boys to direct all their questions about maps and routes to the male counselor; it happened all the time. But whenever Josh noticed it, he would say, "I don't know, ask Tara." The boys would look at him suspiciously, sure that he really did know. But he refused to answer and made them ask me instead.

It seemed a small courtesy at the time—but in all the years since then I've not worked with another man who deliberately took a step back in order to address the inequality in traditional gender roles. When I think of it now, it seems huge.

We skied into the camp basin over New Year's Eve one year. It blizzarded three days straight (surprisingly fun to be stranded) and when the weather cleared we had to break trail back to the car—seven miles through snow that, on skis, came nearly to our waists. Josh pulled a groin muscle partway back, so I took the lead. He didn't complain, he didn't once say how much pain he was in, he muscled through silently. But at one point I looked back and there were tears streaming down his face. Still, he didn't say a word.

Sid the Squid. Ruffles potato chips. George Clinton: Do Fries Go with that Shake? He was willing to do any skit, wear any crazy costume, to make the kids laugh.

And the sticker on his insulated coffee mug that read: "Eschew Obfuscation"

The Shasta trips. How many times did Josh climb that mountain? I went with him twice. He seemed to take special delight in convincing newbies that we could, indeed, climb this huge and intimidating mountain. Before you knew it, you were on a glacier in the pre-dawn dark, ice axe in hand, crampons on your boots, inching slowly upward. Eventually the sun arced out of that darkness and flooded the plains with golden light and you would be overcome with this exhilarating feeling of standing *on top of the world*. And Josh would be grinning at you.

I'm not the first person to say that he had a way of making you feel like you could do almost anything. I sometimes think Josh had more faith in us than he ever had in himself. I know he believed in me far more than I did back then.

And the letters written in beautiful calligraphy script; his Santa on skis cards. Mail from Josh was always good mail.

I hadn't seen him since I moved away from California, more than ten years now. Back then he had been readjusting to life in the Bay Area after years in Colorado, but he joked about it in a very shy way, laughing even when things were hard.

That's what I'll remember the most: his laughter, wit, and unexpected kindness. I'm still so sad, but I'm trying to tell myself he's just gone ahead down the trail a bit; that he's scouting out a good campsite for us all.

I'd really like that to be true.

~ *Tara Austen Weaver*

LITTLE MARSHY LAKE LOT, 1960'S
RITA LOMPA, SUBMITTED BY KIM GARCIA

Sunny days bring joy
Rain, wind and gray skies
Means gloom
Waterfall roaring
Babbling brook and
Marshy Lake
Tents and chairs set up
Toilet, sink and a
Gas stove
Gushing spring water
Big firepit and
Warming fires
Great meals and
S'mores
Family and friends
All joyful
Memories Treasured

In Memory of Roy and Rita Lompa, Marshy Lake lot

Dan, Kim, and Eva write, "Our mom and dad, Roy and Rita Lompa, were among the original lot owners. They bought the Little Marshy Lake lot in the early 1960s. Our dad and Mr. Green were responsible for creating and maintaining the road to Camp and all of the lots for many, many years. Our dad, Roy, served on the board back in the early days of Camp. Our mom, Rita, and all five of us kids would spend the entire summer at Little Marshy while dad was working. Although none of us kids ever attended Camp, we enjoyed running into the troops over the years and still do! Our sister named her son Trinity, so you can see how dear this community is to our hearts."

71

SHARING A LOVE FOR LIFE OUTSIDE
JAMES CAMP, 1945-2018

Testimony of James Camp before the House Public Lands Subcommittee in San Francisco, April 15, 1982

MR. CHAIRMAN, Congressman Miller,

I am James Camp. I live in Humboldt County, where I am a general contractor. For the past dozen years I have been associated with Camp Unalayee in Trinity County..

The House Bills HR 4083,... and HR 5603 are part of an ongoing effort to revise and complete the mandates of the original Wilderness Act.

HR 5603, deceptively called the "Wilderness Protection Act of 1982," is designed to lessen protections already afforded wilderness and wilderness study areas, and it would cut short efforts to see some of this nation's finest lands included in the Wilderness Preservation System."

JAMES' testimony continued on: encompassing the dangerous setbacks to the wilderness system as a whole being imposed by the U.S Forest Service's current RARE II recommendations; exposing loopholes in the HR 5603 bill that would take from Congress and give to the president too much authority over wilderness designations; and also sharing the long held, and now increasingly strong, public sentiments of the local Trinity County supervisors and citizens in northern California that were in favor of the creation of a Trinity Alps Wilderness designation.

James always understood politics and how to remember to praise the powers that be:

"... I think everyone appreciates the work of your subcommittee and the overwhelming support of the House in passing HR 4083. (this was CA Representative Phil Burton's California Wilderness Bill)..It can only be hoped that those in the current administration and those few senators who now block the passage of Senate Bill 1584 (the Senate version) will begin to listen to their counterparts in the House and to the people of California. Thank you."

WHEN I FIRST MET JAMES CAMP IN 1980, he was sitting in the Lake Camp meadow, and I noticed right away his strong, grounded presence and his beautiful, gentle voice. Soon after, we had our first conversation in the Central Meadow looking at a full view of Bear Ridge (although the view is now obscured by the trees, there's a big peridotite rock there which is a great backrest, and it was always our favorite dinner spot at Family Camp in later years).

That day, James wanted to talk about The Trinity Wilderness Coalition (TWC) : "Was I interested in helping with their efforts to preserve the Trinity Primitive Area? I was a graduate of Stanford, right? Maybe I'd like to help in some way? They are having hearings."

LATELY I'VE BEEN READING about people famous for their work in pushing forward the Environmental Movement of the mid-1900's (think: David Brower, Ansel Adams, Martin Litton, Rachel Carson, Huey Johnson, Howard Zahniser, Paul and Anne Erlich...). Good times exploring in the wild outdoors with friends gave many of them their passion for Conservation, Preservation, and Restoration ("CPR" -David Brower's acronym) of Earth's natural resources and wild places. Like so many of the prominent environmental leaders before him, I think a lifetime of studying and recreating outdoors affected James in the same way.

" THERE IS *a lot to be learned from climbing mountains, more than you might think, about life, about saving the Earth, and not a little about both.*

...mountains build bold leaders, many of whom in the early days, came down from the mountains to save them."
David Brower

. . .

As soon as he was 18, James lived as much as possible in the outdoors: learning the flowers in the Santa Cruz mountains; backpacking and rock-climbing in the Sierras; and learning about the southern California deserts while working at a Girl Scouts summer camp. Once he was introduced to Camp Unalayee at age 23, he spent his first decade there in various roles: being a Central Tribe cook; leading arts and crafts; increasing and sharing his knowledge of botany (James drafted the layout for a Nature Center he dreamed could become part of the craft shack); educating interested older campers in the need for "CPR" of wildlands (a program called The Environmental Forum); leading Wild Tribes (fun with Lowell and Corinne); being a Director, and always extensively exploring the backcountry of the Klamath-Siskiyou mountains with kids and on his own trips.

"CONSERVATION (FINDS) *its way into (your) blood at high altitude*"
    Tom Turner

By 1980, James had already spent over 15 years in the high-altitude backcountry climbing rocks and camping in forests of various wildernesses. His strong Unalayee connection led him to working with TWC to help protect the wilderness of the Trinity Alps Primitive Area and its adjoining lands. RARE II and the future roads and resource extraction it might allow on public lands loomed large. (I remember, after my first summer living at 6500' with the forests and rocks of the ancient Scott Mts, the gut punch I felt seeing the logging along Hwy 3 upon leaving Camp. I was ready to sign up with Earth First!)

At the time of James' testimony begun above (full version is available if you are interested), the Reagan Administration-with the infamous Interior Secretary Watt-had imperiled beautiful wildlands all over the USA. In the Salmon-Trinity Alps, the threats to areas like the Scott Mountains and The Russians falling prey to the timber industry and the Forest Service's mismanagement were mounting. These areas had been left out of a California Wilderness Act bill -now awaiting Senate approval- because not enough people knew their essential value to the Trinity Alps region. TWC was trying to build a coalition of knowledgeable supporters who had seen and could reliably champion them.

James joined the effort because he wanted to protect the area he had grown to love, and he also had just the right kind of *manner* to convincingly testify at a hearing: grounded, pointedly assured, yet complimentary... you know the voice. He had cut his hair. The only thing he lacked was a proper pair of shoes. For the rest of his life, his dress shoes were what we called his "Hearing shoes." He acquired them for that purpose, and they served him more than well.

Ultimately, in 1984 The California Wilderness Act passed, and it included protection for The Scotts and The Russians. California's Senator Alan Cranston had been taken up into Swift Creek and Bear Basin by TWC to see what he was being asked to save. Like when President Teddy Roosevelt was taken to Yosemite by John Muir in 1903 because,

It's hard to want to save what you don't know.

And that simple fact is what led James to spend the next 35 years of his life working in Environmental Education. We founded **Fieldguides Inc.** in 1983 because, having been enamored of Unalayee's summer camp style, we wanted more kids -via their schools' science field trips- to know what it was like to live *outside* for several days (no cabins, tent platforms, cafeterias, swimming pools, bus trips..). To sleep on the ground.

"To go in the dark with a light is to know the light. To know the dark, go dark."
Wendell Berry

I WANTED to call the organization *Wildways,* but James felt that it was better to gently coax people into the outdoors. If it sounded too wild, school districts might not sign up. So, *Fieldguides.* Together with our friends we would "guide" them into learning to feel safe outside in our company, to like sleeping on the ground and all that comes with outdoor living; and finally to know that the "wild" places were treasures worth saving. Today, in a year, over 1,000 kids and adults continue to have their first experience in the outdoors at *Fieldguides'* programs.

Meanwhile, of course his summers at Unalayee were always James' favorite pastime. In myriad ways James continued to nurture old and new friends and share his love for wilderness: leading staff hikes, trail tribes, CIT tribes, regular tribes, telling stargazing and campfire stories, mentoring work and building crews, restoring the beaten down high traffic areas, and always, keeping on learning the flowers. James ended up spending 50 summers at Unalayee. He is remembered for his gentle soul, inviting and affable manner with both newcomers and generations of campers and staff, and the craft shack and food shack he joyfully designed and built with friends.

What was under the surface was always his love of living in the great outdoors and from this came his devotion to a life of conservation, preservation and restoration of our natural resources. Looking back at a year spent working at

Unalayee, backpacking in wilderness, and running Fieldguides programs, he always liked to count the number of nights he'd slept "on the ground." He found great happiness in always reaching numbers in the hundreds.

David Brower is considered by many to be the *archdruid* of active environmentalism in the 20th Century. Brower, a mountaineer with great intellect and vision, was successful in saving wild places all over the world. This was in large part because he was able to genuinely befriend and inspire *others* to work hard with him in the effort. Although in a smaller sphere of influence, I feel like James had a similar gift.

In the words of Brower's grandson: *"He was this big, big figure with a gentle voice."*

~ Sarah Priestman

72

A GREAT GAME
JAMES CAMP

James Camp is up early, down in Central, engaged in a work crew project. His wife Jessie, and daughter Sarah, are out on a "Girls Getaway" hike, and his son, Galen, gets up alone at their "spot," behind Lake 3. Galen is perhaps five years old, convinced he is Peter Pan, and not upset or afraid of waking up alone. Camp, much like Neverland, is home, a beautiful, pristine, subalpine playground all for him (and his lost boys). Making his way to Central he grabs a sword (stick) and, man-to-flower, with one hand behind his back, begins lopping off the tops of Common Groundsels. He regrets this action later in life, but at the time, as a skilled swordsman, his stroke is (truly) deadly.

Galen makes his way past the Lake 1 Meadow, tossing his saber aside, the flowers gone - beheaded the day before. Careless, he eases his way down the Craft Shack Hill. Suddenly, there is movement in the deer brush by the Central campfire, a snarl, a rustle, and the brave warrior Galen, without weapon, freezes, gathers his wits, and.... flies, screaming and crying for his father all the way to Central.

Spinning around the Chalet's work bench, peering through teary eyes, Galen finally sees his father. James comes jogging up, arms open, and embraces his son. The savior, the comforter, calm, gentle, James Camp.

When I think of my father, I often think of this demeanor, the gentle giant. Rosemary Shanahan, a teacher at Fieldguides, once told my family that when parents were nervous about sending their kids on an overnight, she would explain that the man running the organization was like the, "Mr. Rogers of the Wilderness." I have always loved that comparison, I think it represents him well.

James had a way of reassuring others, connecting with people and making them feel seen, and safe. I often picture him, standing, both arms behind his back, with one hand clasping the opposite wrist. Courteous, calm, accommodating.

I want to depart from this picture of James, with arms behind his back, and return to the picture in our story, with arms wrapped around his son. Maybe I want to revisit what I can no longer have, stay wrapped in his arms, his love, a small boy in Neverland, forever and ever, safe. But there is more to the story.

He reassures his son, "You're okay, you're safe, everything is okay. There isn't anything in the bushes, that was just *me*. I was coming up to check on you and I saw you walking down. I thought I would surprise you. I didn't mean to scare you."

This was also James. The playful, mischievous, adventurous. I imagine those of you who knew him in his youth saw this side of him regularly. I've heard stories. Tom Buoye telling how he created the "Wild Tribe," and made the qualifications for leading it ones only he had. Lowell Fitch relating a winter snow adventure, the two of them trapped outside at night without sleeping bags and walking in a circle until dawn to stay warm. I know from past fliers that in the early days of Fieldguides he and my mom offered a *"beginners"* backpacking trip through Grizzly and Mirror. For those of you who haven't been, I would not call that a *"beginners"* hike.

Staff in younger generations have also experienced this side of James. I recall Dion Shaughnessy telling me how James recommended dropping straight down from Smith Lake to Morris Meadows. A route I'm told ranges from technical, to terrifying. He also gave me questionable route advice. It turns out cross countrying from Shadow Lake over the southside and down into the ABCD Lakes, is not viable for 13-year-olds with trail packs. I found that out the hard, and very long, way. Did he do it all from some mischievous place? Was it truly easy for him? Or did the dream of adventure make anything seem possible?

As a family we watched the movie *Hook* many, many times. Robin Williams plays a middle-aged Peter Pan, turned joyless businessman, returning to Neverland to find his kids and himself. Near the end of the movie, as Peter flies away, one of the lost boys watches him go and says, "That was a great game." James loved this line. After a long day of work, or play, he would sometimes recite, "That was a great game, Peter."

James played a great game, with wonderful people, in a beautiful place. Caring, adventurous, and full of love. I can't help but see his same qualities in the community he found at Unalayee. The community he shared with his family. The community that continues to share with me, stories, wilderness, friendship. While Camp's community may age, and the basin change, much like Neverland, Camp stays young. New generations continue being sprinkled with its magical

Jeffrey Pine dust, allowing them a moment in time to fly; ageless, adventurous, safe. All of us at Camp are held safe in that basin, by memory, community, and people like James, arms behind his back, yet somehow embracing the whole world.

Sometimes I still spin in circles by the lake at night, peering up through teary eyes at the stars. And while James is no longer there to wraps me in his arms, I am held, by the breeze, the gentle smell of evergreens, and memory that sends me upward and onward, "past the second star to the right, and straight on 'til morning."

THANK you for taking the time to read and remember my father. If you knew him, or would like to know me better, then I would also like to know you better and welcome a future conversation, story, or memory. ~ Galen Camp

73

JAMES CAMP

RIP my old friend, mentor, teacher, colleague, James Camp. James was one of my earliest teachers of outdoor skills and leadership, he was my instructor when I was a sixteen year-old counselor-in-training. He gave me a foundation in wilderness living and travel that has served me my whole life. He taught me knots, he taught me map and compass, shelter-building, and fire starting. He taught me how to read the weather and the landscape and the stars. He taught me how to lead groups effectively under adverse conditions.

But I also learned many other life lessons from him over the years, as I moved from trainee to co-worker, from child to adult. From James, I learned:

- that strength is best projected quietly
- that toughness and gentleness are not mutually exclusive, but best practiced together
- that patience can be a power in itself
- that however improbable it looks from the ground, that route goes.

May your trails be wild and steep, old friend. Safe passage. I will miss you.
~ *Fred Lifton*

74

SCOTT COSGROVE
1964-2016

Scott was tall and long-limbed, destined to be a climber. His eyes reflected the lively spirit and generous nature of someone who spends a lot of time on rocks in high places.

James Camp and I were always proud of our hiking skills. Competitive, racing to the top of ridges with Jay Watson or Tom Buoye. Scott humbled us:

I remember doing a staff hike with Scott in the 80's sometime. We went to South Fork Lake and the agenda was to climb "7794," the peak above the lake. We all started, taking the routes we thought were best. James and I were in the front group of staff and thought for sure we'd be first to the top. As we got higher and could see the top, choosing a route that avoided too much brush, or especially exposure, someone was already there! Sure enough, it was Scott. He had been there, he said, probably about 30 minutes or so. By all we could tell, not only did he have great speed, but he had to have scaled a cliffy section that wasn't in any of our comfort zones.

That was when I realized what a mountain goat Scott was, and I wasn't surprised to hear that after Unalayee years, he saved lives working for Search and Rescue in Yosemite, evacuating stranded rock climbers from scary places.

~ *Jessie Camp*

75

CARMEN DIAZ
1955-2019

My sister and I were 11 (me) and 10. We were put alone on a Greyhound bus from the Bay Area and had no idea what was next. Six hours and one rest stop in Redding later, we were in a carved out hillside three miles up a dirt road.

And along came Carmen. She was loud, cheery, very talkative, giggly. We were shy, tired and trying not to cry. She told us not to worry about our stuff and we, along with around 8 other little kids, started walking, and walking, and walking. It was unknown, no one told us what to expect and I just remember hating it.

And there was Carmen, talking and laughing and joking and talking some more. Walking so easily while we struggled. And then finally she said "We're HERE." There was no here there.

And she laughed. We still had a "mountain" to climb to reach Lake 1 - this time with our bags. The first night is kind of a blur and a very long time ago. But I clearly remember that even though we were out of sorts and all turned around, Carmen was our light.

Our session at Camp was OK because we had her. We couldn't bear to leave her and so tackled a Choice Hike to Bear Lake as jake campers because the alternative was to go with someone else. She was beautiful and fierce. She didn't know my life, but this is JUST what I needed at that time. And in the end, I cried and cried. I promised I would come back, and I did.

But before I did, Carmen reached out. This led to a visit to her home. Christmas cookie baking at her house. An escape from my life that I can never thank her enough for. Carmen was truly the best. I will always remember her. Her laugh. Her living example of the badass woman I wanted to be.

~Erica (Arteseros) Brown

I spent 7 years as a camper and 10 years as a counselor. After a break, I returned to work-crew for another 10 years. Work has gotten in the way of being at Camp, but my heart and funds still contribute to this beautiful community that helped raise me. I am currently in the San Francisco Fire Department, working first as a firefighter, a community response team builder and now the Chief of our FD homeland security division on the command staff.

76

CAROLINE REEVES JOHNSON
1948-2016

In 1974 Caroline Johnson, nee Reeves, and I were both hired for the first time to work at Camp Unalayee. She went on the first true wild tribe, summit to summit hike with James Camp and Bill Moss. I got to know her later that summer and we became best friends. We shared many adventures at Unalayee, in the Trinities, in the Sierra Nevada and Colorado mountains, and rafting down the Grand Canyon with her husband Mac Johnson and children Tessa and Milo. Not to mention the ski races she entered me in every time I visited them in Durango, CO. I once finished 2nd. 2nd to last, an improvement.

There are so many adventures and memories that I have of her and I'll try and share a couple here.

- She and I once swapped pairs of Levi's in 1975
- She gave me a copy of W*inds of War,* perhaps the greatest historical novel about WW II. I bought the sequel, *War and Remembrance* the day it was issued..
- The Hubris of Holland Lake - Thanks, Mac, for suggesting the name, which I'll briefly recap here.

10 TO 20 YEARS AGO, Caroline, Mac and I thought we would go to Holland lake from Camp. Early in the AM we hiked down to the gate, drove to the Stoddard

Lake trailhead and headed out. It was lunchtime and so we left Stoddard at about 3 pm.

Four or 5 hours later, we were on the traverse above McDonald and the puddles. I was out of water and exhausted. Caroline asked and was astounded that I had no idea where Holland was. You should have seen the look on her face, as she assumed I had been there.

We made it back to the puddle and made dinner by headlight. Pure ego, pure hubris.

I miss her very much.

~ *Tom Buoye*

77

MAY OUR STORIES CONTINUE...

Mosquito Creek

Rose Lee, age 6

www.ingramcontent.com/pod-product-compliance
Lightning Source LLC
Chambersburg PA
CBHW030443090526
44586CB00044B/580